THE COMPLETE
HUNTER™

HUNTING
in North America

●●●●●●●●●●●●●●●●●

Big Game • Small Game
Upland Birds • Waterfowl
Wild Turkey

CREATIVE
PUBLISHING
international

MINNETONKA, MINNESOTA

CREDITS

Creative Publishing international, Inc.
5900 Green Oak Drive
Minnetonka, MN 55343
1-800-328-3895

President/CEO: David D. Murphy
Vice President/Editorial: Patricia K. Jacobsen
Vice President/Retail Sales & Marketing: Richard M. Miller

HUNTING IN NORTH AMERICA

Executive Editor, Outdoor Group: Don Oster
Editorial Director: David R. Maas
Senior Editor: David L. Tieszen
Managing Editor: Jill Anderson
Project Manager: Tracy Stanley
Creative Director: Brad Springer
Senior Art Director: Dave Schelitzche
Art Director: Joe Fahey
Photo Researcher: Angela Hartwell
Director, Production Services: Kim Gerber
Production Manager: Helga Thielen
Production Staff: Laura Hokkanen, Kay Swanson
Copy Editor: Shannon Zemlicka

Contributing Photographers: Charles J. Alsheimer, Denver Bryan, Kathy Butt, Judd Cooney, Jeff Foott / Tom Stack & Associates, Victoria Hurst / Tom Stack & Associates, Donald M. Jones, Thomas Kitchin / Tom Stack & Associates, Gary Kramer, Bill Lea, Stephen W. Maas, Bill Marchel, Robert McCaw, Bill McRae, Arthur Morris / BIRDS AS ART, Scott Nielsen, Debi Ottinger, Bob Robb, John Shaw / Tom Stack & Associates, Ron Spomer, Diana L. Stratton / Tom Stack & Associates, Tom Walker

Printed on American paper by: R. R. Donnelley & Sons Co.
10   9   8   7   6   5   4   3   2   1

Library of Congress Cataloging-in-Publication Data

Hunting in North America: big game, small game, upland game birds, waterfowl, wild turkey.
    p.cm. -- (The Complete hunter)
    ISBN 0-86573-120-9 (softcover)
    1. Hunting--North America. I. Creative Publishing International. II. Complete hunter (Creative Publishing International)
    SK40 .H866 2000
    799.297--dc21   00-022689

CONTENTS

INTRODUCTION

Whether you pursue elk in the Rockies or squirrels in a thicket near your home, the sport of hunting offers a unique challenge. You must outsmart a wild animal that has a better knowledge of its environment and more highly developed senses than your own.

This challenge, along with the camaraderie that goes hand in hand with hunting, accounts for the sport's tremendous popularity. And a successful hunter can enjoy a supply of lean, nutritious, untainted meat.

Hunting in North America is intended to make you a better hunter. Each section of the book deals with a different facet of the sport. Together, they will help you develop the skills and savvy needed to consistently bag wild game.

The first section, "All About Wild Game," will improve your understanding of wildlife behavior and help you to recognize good habitat. By knowing how animals sense danger, react to threats, and find food, water and cover, you can improve your chances of being in the right spot at the right time.

"Hunting Skills and Equipment" gives you all the information you need to select rifles, shotguns, bows and arrows, and even muzzleloaders. You will also learn how to choose the best ammunition for the game you hunt and how to become a proficient shooter. This section goes far beyond the basics, explaining complex principles of bullet and shot performance with descriptive photos and easy-to-understand charts.

"Hunting Strategies" gets you started right by showing you how to plan your hunt and how to scout a potential spot to make sure it holds game. This section details the most popular hunting techniques, from stalking to driving. You will learn how to tailor your hunting strategy to the terrain and time of day. The section also provides valuable tips for recovering downed game.

The final section, "Hunting Wild Game," acquaints you with the continent's most popular game animals. The many informative how-to-photos, along with a fact-filled text, help you locate, pursue and bag each of these species.

Astounding photography puts you in the hunting scene. You will experience the spine-tingling thrill of drawing your bow on a trophy whitetail; the pulse-stopping excitement of a ring-necked pheasant bursting from cover at your feet; and the nerve-wracking anticipation of waiting for a wild turkey to strut close enough for a shot.

The hunting techniques shown in this book are those considered most effective by the nation's top hunting authorities. Hunting regulations and legal equipment differ in every state and province, so it is possible that some of the procedures described are illegal in your area. Baiting bears, for instance, is a popular method in some states, but is against the law in others. Check the hunting laws if there is any question on a technique's legality.

In addition to the proven high-percentage hunting methods, this book will also reveal dozens of little-known but effective tips that help the experts take their game. You will learn how to estimate shooting range using the muzzle of your shotgun and how to compensate for wind drift when shooting your rifle.

This book is a unique blend of straightforward writing and captivating photography. Never before has so much how-to hunting information and so many dramatic wildlife photographs been packed into one volume. *Hunting in North America* is sure to make your days afield more enjoyable – and more successful.

1

ALL ABOUT

WILD GAME

Understanding Game Populations

From the moment its life begins, a game animal faces threats from predators, weather, disease and competition from its own kind. Only the strongest and wariest offspring live to reproduce. In this way, nature continually selects the best breeding stock to insure that the species will survive.

All game animals have the potential to produce many more young than the habitat can support. Reproductive rates are especially high among small game and upland birds. High mortality rates are nature's way of keeping game populations in check. When too many animals survive, a population explosion results, causing disease, stunted growth and eventually starvation.

Among most upland birds, waterfowl and small game, 60 to 80 percent of the population dies each year. Individuals

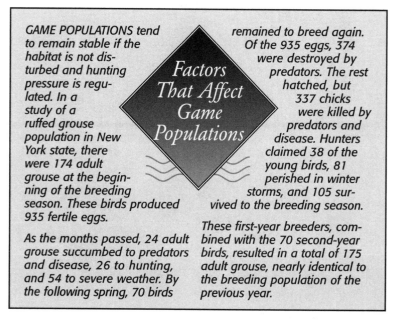

Factors That Affect Game Populations

GAME POPULATIONS tend to remain stable if the habitat is not disturbed and hunting pressure is regulated. In a study of a ruffed grouse population in New York state, there were 174 adult grouse at the beginning of the breeding season. These birds produced 935 fertile eggs.

As the months passed, 24 adult grouse succumbed to predators and disease, 26 to hunting, and 54 to severe weather. By the following spring, 70 birds remained to breed again. Of the 935 eggs, 374 were destroyed by predators. The rest hatched, but 337 chicks were killed by predators and disease. Hunters claimed 38 of the young birds, 81 perished in winter storms, and 105 survived to the breeding season.

These first-year breeders, combined with the 70 second-year birds, resulted in a total of 175 adult grouse, nearly identical to the breeding population of the previous year.

BIG-GAME POPULATIONS can reach high levels despite low reproductive rates. Predators take only an occasional young animal. In areas with good habitat and little hunting pressure, herds may grow so large that food shortages result. Hunting regulations are set to control the harvest, yet prevent overpopulation.

over 1 year old comprise only 20 to 40 percent of the fall population. Because young animals are more abundant and because they lack the savvy of older individuals, they make up the bulk of the hunter's bag.

Big-game populations have a relatively low reproductive potential. The average animal lives longer and fall populations contain a higher percentage of older individuals, usually from 65 to 85 percent.

Hunting regulations are based on the concept that game can be harvested as long as enough breeding stock remains to produce another crop of similar size the following year. Seasons for small game, waterfowl and upland birds are usually long and bag limits generous. Liberal regulations are possible because of the high reproductive rates of these animals. Regulations for big game are stricter because the animals produce fewer young.

Resource agencies closely monitor game populations and set regulations to achieve the desired harvest. Modern management has eliminated the problems of mass slaughter associated with market hunting in years past. In fact, some of the continent's major game species, such as whitetail deer and wild turkey, are more numerous today than at any time in recorded history.

Senses of Game Animals

VOCAL SIGNALS are used by animals to attract mates, to alert each other to danger, to rally their young after a predator attack, to mark territories and to intimidate other males during the breeding season.

Game animals have an amazing ability to elude hunters. Their keen senses of sight, smell and hearing enable them to detect danger far in advance and take evasive action. Many animals also possess unique survival adaptations that far exceed the capabilities of humans.

Hunters who understand the senses and special adaptations of the game they pursue stand the best chance of success.

SIGHT. Game birds have color vision that may surpass that of humans. Their retinas have more color receptors, or *cones*, than most other game animals. Colored oil droplets in the retina work like a camera filter, enhancing the visibility of certain hues. The cones also give them excellent *visual acuity*, or sharpness.

Game mammals have retinas that contain mostly light receptors, or *rods*. The rods enable them to see well in dim light. Night vision in nocturnal animals is enhanced by the *tapetum lucidum*, a layer of reflective pigment below the surface of the retina. Light passes through the receptors on the retina's surface, hits the tapetum, then bounces back to stimulate the receptors again.

The vision of most game mammals is not as sharp as that of birds or humans (see chart p. 12), and they have limited color vision. In one study, whitetail deer were rewarded with a drink from a tube when a red light went on; a white light gave no reward. Even though the lights switched between two tubes, deer consistently made the right choice.

Most mammals have poor *accommodation* capabilities; they cannot change the shape of their lenses to focus on both close and distant objects. As a result, images are often fuzzy. This explains why many types of big-game animals do not seem to notice a stationary hunter.

SMELL. Game mammals collect most of the information about their environment through their sense of smell. In a laboratory test, rabbits were able to detect the smell of acetone at a concentration of only 1/50th of that detectable by humans. Hunters who pursue big or small game should try to approach from downwind to keep their scent from drifting toward the animals.

Game birds have a poor sense of smell. In one study, wild turkey were given two piles of grain, one of which contained a highly repulsive scent. The birds paid no attention to the odor, feeding equally at each pile. To a bird in flight, a highly-developed sense of smell would be of little value because odors produced by predators quickly sink to the ground.

Some big-game animals position themselves below the crest of a wind-swept ridge, which enables them to smell anything approaching from above. They watch for anything coming from below. Scent glands warn other animals of danger. For

COMPARING THE SENSES OF MAN TO GAME ANIMALS

	VISION	HEARING	SMELL
Man	Good	Good	Fair
Whitetail Deer	Fair	Excellent	Excellent
Cottontail Rabbit	Good	Excellent	Good
Wild Turkey	Excellent	Excellent	Poor
Ring-Necked Pheasant	Good	Good	Poor
Mallard Duck	Excellent	Good	Fair

example, when a mule deer faces a threat, *metatarsal glands* on the hind leg produce an odor that alerts other herd members. Animals will also freeze in position and press their body to the ground to reduce the amount of scent they give off. Some game birds also compress their feathers so less scent escapes.

HEARING. Because birds lack external ears and because their ears have fewer small bones than those of mammals, they are not as well-equipped for detecting faint sounds. And because the ears are close together, they are not as well-suited to locating the direction of sounds. The range of pitches they can recognize is slightly less than that of humans, and substantially less than that of many game mammals.

Exposed ears gather sound waves. They also help an animal pinpoint the source of a sound by the difference in the time it takes for the signal to reach each ear. Movable external ears enable mammals to locate sounds from any direction. While one ear detects a sound from one direction, the other picks up a sound from a different source.

In a test of their ability to detect various pitches, mallards recognized sounds up to a frequency of 8000 cycles per second (cps). Humans detected higher pitched sounds, up to 20,000 cps, and raccoons heard sounds of up to 85,000 cps.

SPECIAL ADAPTATIONS. The process of evolution has provided almost every type of game animal with some unique physical feature or ability that gives it an advantage over other animals. These adaptations enable the species to survive the threats posed by predators, including man.

Many of these adaptations are so foreign to humans that we fail to consider them when hunting. For example, a mallard can stay submerged for as long as 16 minutes. It accomplishes this seemingly impossible feat by slowing its heart rate by more than 50 percent while underwater. This substantially reduces its oxygen needs.

Many a hunter has winged a duck, marked it down, spent 5 to 10 minutes looking for it, then given up in frustration. After the hunter returns to the blind, the duck appears in the very spot it went down.

TYPES OF SPECIAL ADAPTATIONS

•*Flared rump hair* alerts other animals to a threat. By flaring its rump hairs to the side, the pronghorn can greatly increase the size and visibility of its white rump patch.

• *Camouflage* enables game animals to escape detection by predators. The woodcock blends in so well with vegetation that it can hide in open terrain with no overhead cover.

•*Genetic changes* may result from hunting. The tendency to run has increased among pheasants. Many hunters attribute this to the fact that fliers get shot, leaving runners to breed.

Wildlife Habitat

Good habitat is the key to wildlife abundance. Game animals need year-round cover and a reliable supply of food. Many also require drinking water on a regular basis, although some get sufficient water from their food or can go without for long periods.

The best wildlife habitat has a variety of plant life. A mixed plant community generally supports more species and higher numbers of game than an expanse of the same type of vegetation.

Most types of game find the necessary plant variety along the edge between two vegetative types. Where a forest meets a marsh, for instance, the mixture of grasses, berry bushes, low-growing leafy plants and young trees provide an excellent supply of food and cover. The area where the two types of vegetation meet usually holds more kinds and higher numbers of game than either type by itself. This principle is known as the *edge effect.*

Another factor that influences plant variety is *succession.* For example, after a forest fire or logging operation, the bare ground almost immediately begins to grow grasses, shrubs and trees. As the trees grow taller, they begin to form a canopy that shades the forest floor. As the canopy grows denser, shrubs and grasses disappear because of the lack of sunlight. Eventually, only large trees remain. These changes in the plant community invariably affect the type and amount of game the habitat can support.

Succession begins after trees have been removed. New grasses, shrubs and trees support animals like whitetail deer. As time goes on, trees grow taller, yet enough sunlight penetrates to promote a dense growth of underbrush ideal for animals like ruffed grouse. As the trees mature and shade out the forest floor, underbrush disappears and the forest becomes best suited for animals like black bear.

Wildlife managers often set back the process of succession by periodically cutting or burning forested areas to promote growth of new vegetation. These techniques enable them to increase the production of important game species.

In most agricultural areas, the trend is toward less habitat variety. Many farms once had small, weedy cropfields combined with brushy fencelines, unmowed roadside ditches, large wetlands and dense groves. Today's clean farms have vast acreages of crops unbroken by fencelines, wetlands or trees. Even roadside ditches are often mowed for hay. These intensive agricultural practices severely reduce or eliminate populations of farmland game like pheasants and bobwhite quail.

Wildlife Habitat: Cover

To many hunters, the term *cover* means a well-hidden spot where animals can escape danger. And it is true that escape cover is vital to the survival of almost every game species. But most wildlife also needs other kinds of cover for bedding, loafing, protection from the elements, and producing young.

A ring-necked pheasant, for example, often escapes from hunters by hiding in dense brush. It may roost in open grasslands, loaf along the grassy margin of a cropfield and burrow under a clump of slough grass during a storm. Experienced hunters know where to look at different times of the day and under different weather conditions.

ESCAPE COVER. Predators pose a constant threat to most game animals. Wildlife must learn to contend with these threats, or perish. Most elude predators by hiding in dense cover; others scamper to a burrow or den; in light cover, some crouch motionless or rely on camouflage.

BEDDING COVER. Some game animals bed in dens or burrows, or roost in trees. Others prefer thick grassy cover for bedding sites. The grass offers concealment and warns animals of danger. Even the stealthiest predator would have difficulty moving through thick grass without making some noise.

LOAFING COVER. Most game animals feed heavily in early morning and late afternoon, then loaf during midday. Loafing cover is thick enough so that animals are not easily visible, but not so dense that they cannot see.

COVER FROM THE ELEMENTS. All game animals need some type of dense cover to insulate them from extremely cold temperatures. They also use cover as shelter from precipitation, strong winds and the hot summer sun.

Many birds and small mammals crawl under vegetation to escape harsh winter storms. Some burrow under the snow, creating a cozy enclosure. The animal's body heat may keep the temperature as much as 50 degrees warmer than the outside air. Big-game animals may bed down under conifer limbs in a heavy rain or on a cold night. The boughs shed precipitation and act like a blanket to slow the loss of body heat into the atmosphere.

PRODUCTION COVER. Predators and adverse weather will quickly wipe out nesting adults and newly-produced young unless they have good production cover. This type of cover may not hold animals during the hunting season, but it often serves as an indicator of high game populations.

Wildlife Habitat: Food and Water

Hunters who understand the feeding habits and water needs of their quarry can better predict its daily movements. This makes it easier to select a good hunting location.

An elk may travel miles to find food or quench its thirst, but most wildlife needs food and water in close proximity to cover. If an animal has to travel a long distance across open terrain to fulfill these basic needs, it is more visible to predators.

FOOD. Most game animals can adapt to a wide variety of foods. Researchers have found that bobwhite quail consume over 1000 different foods including seeds, plants, nuts and insects.

Despite their ability to use such a wide range of foods, most animals select items that they can digest easily and that are high in proteins and calories.

They seem to instinctively know which foods are most nutritious. In one study, squirrels gained weight when fed a diet consisting solely of white oak acorns. But they lost weight when fed acorns of red oak. In nature, squirrels commonly feed on acorns of white oak, but ignore those of red oak.

Like humans, game animals must have vitamins and minerals in their diet. Most animals obtain these vital elements from their food and water, but some need additional salt. They frequent springs and natural soil deposits with high salt contents. Many birds pick up grit not only to grind their food, but to provide needed minerals.

SOURCES OF WILDLIFE FOOD

•*Natural foods* are the mainstay in the diets of most game animals. A good supply of winter food is especially critical. Survival rates are generally low in years when winter food is scarce.

•*Food plots* planted by wildlife agencies provide an additional source of food during winter, when natural food may be difficult to find. Some farmers leave a few rows of corn to sustain wildlife on their land.

•*Waste grain* remains after farmers harvest their crops. It provides a temporary food supply for many animals like geese, ducks, pheasants and deer. They gather in large numbers to take advantage of this easy source of food. Waste grain may provide food throughout the winter where fields are left unplowed.

WATER. Birds generally require less water than mammals, because they can reuse water as it passes through their digestive tract. Gambel's quail, for example, can go a month or two without visiting a water hole. Pronghorns, on the other hand, need water each day.

Many game species can survive in areas with no lakes, streams or other sources of surface water. They obtain water from foods or dew.

SOURCES OF WATER

•*Surface water* is a requirement for many kinds of game. Popular watering sites include streams, lakes, man-made ponds and natural springs.

•*Succulent foods,* like prickly pear cactus, provide water in arid climates. Rabbits and grouse often get water from grasses and buds.

•*Frost or dew* also provides water in dry climates. To use this water source, animals must feed in early morning before the plants dry off.

Wildlife Habitat: Common Types

Some game animals can adapt to almost any kind of habitat. Whitetail deer, for instance, live in places as diverse as Florida swamps, southwestern deserts and mountains of the Pacific Northwest. But most types of wildlife have much more specific habitat requirements.

When hunting in unfamiliar territory, it pays to spend a

good deal of time scouting. Conditions may not be right for spotting game, but you can always recognize good habitat.

Many types of wildlife have cover, food or water needs so specific that merely finding a broad habitat type is not enough. For example, moose prefer young conifer-hardwood forests. But within these forests, they seldom stray far from streambanks, lakeshores or willow bogs, their main feeding sites. Sage grouse live in semi-arid brushlands, but rarely venture more than one-half mile from a water hole or other source of water.

As the seasons change, many species of game migrate to different types of habitat. In late fall, waterfowl leave northern marshes en masse. Most winter in the South, resting and feeding on large lakes and in cropfields. As winter approaches, some types of mountain wildlife migrate to lower elevations, wintering in grasslands that offer more food and a less severe climate.

Hunting pressure may also force animals from their pre-ferred habitat. Elk favor grassy mountain meadows, but when hunters begin to invade their territory, they retreat to higher, more rugged terrain where a man on foot could not follow. Waterfowl abandon many small lakes and ponds once the season opens. They seek refuge in the open water of large lakes and reservoirs.

In agricultural areas, wildlife may have to use other cover once crops are harvested. Pheasant hunters usually find the birds in cropfields during early season. But when the crops are removed, the birds move to permanent heavy cover like cattail swamps and woodlots.

Throughout this book, we will identify the habitats most commonly associated with each species of game.

2

HUNTING SKILLS AND

EQUIPMENT

The Hunting Rifle

A rifle that suits your style of hunting greatly increases your chances of success. When selecting a rifle, consider its action, weight and caliber.

ACTION. The action refers to the design of the mechanism for chambering ammunition and ejecting spent cartridges. Single-shot actions, like the *falling block*, are extremely reliable because they have few moving parts. Their rigid mechanisms hold the cartridge firmly, resulting in a high degree of accuracy. These rifles must be reloaded after each round is fired, so they teach shooters to make the first shot count.

Repeating actions hold several cartridges in the magazine, making it possible to fire more than one shot without

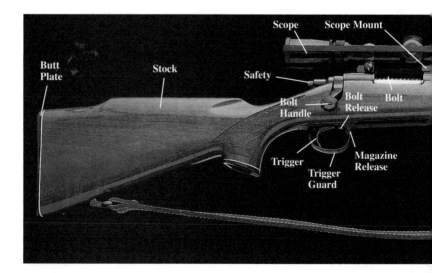

reloading. Like single shots, *bolt* actions have a rigid design and few moving parts. With a bolt action, a spring forces a cartridge out of the magazine when the bolt is drawn back. When pushed forward, the bolt seats a cartridge in the chamber. Pulling the trigger causes the firing pin to strike the cartridge primer, igniting the powder. Drawing the bolt back extracts the spent cartridge. Many hunters consider the bolt action to be the most accurate and reliable rifle. *Lever, pump* and *semi-automatic* actions are designed for faster firing. You may need a quick second shot if you fail to kill the animal or if a branch deflects your bullet. But fast-action rifles have more moving parts, increasing the chance of mechanical failure, especially in cold weather or when dirt gets into the action.

WEIGHT. Rifles commonly weigh between 6 and 9 pounds without cartridges, slings or scopes. The recoil, or *kick,* of a rifle depends mainly on its weight and its cartridge/caliber combination. Within a given combination, a heavy rifle has the least recoil, because the weight absorbs much of the energy that would otherwise be transmitted to your shoulder. Heavy rifles are easiest to hold steady and generally result in more accurate shots. Light rifles are easier to carry over a long distance.

The term *carbine* denotes a light rifle with a short barrel.

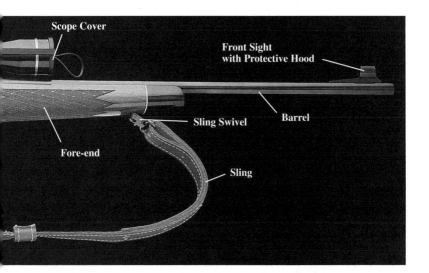

Scope Cover

Front Sight
with Protective Hood

Barrel

Sling Swivel

Fore-end

Sling

Some hunters prefer carbines when hunting in heavy cover, where a longer rifle would tend to catch on brush or tree limbs.

CALIBER. The *caliber* of a rifle refers to the diameter of the barrel opening, or *bore*. Caliber is measured in hundredths or thousandths of an inch, or in millimeters. Hunters use rifles as small as .17 caliber for small animals and rifles up to .458 caliber for big game. Many rifle models are available in a choice of several calibers. Within a particular model of bolt action there may be 15 different calibers.

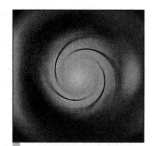

RIFLING GROOVES in the barrel cause the bullet to spin rapidly. The spinning motion makes the bullet travel smoothly without wobbling, much like a spiraling football.

Hunters are often confused by traditional caliber designations. A .30-06 rifle has a .30-inch diameter bore. The 06 refers to 1906, the year the rifle was introduced. A .30-30 rifle also shoots a .30 caliber bullet. The bullet was originally propelled by 30 grains of smokeless powder. To further complicate the matter, some caliber designations do not refer to the diameter of the bore. For example, the bore of a .308 Winchester rifle does not measure .308 inch. The .308 refers to the *groove diameter*, or the diameter to the outside of the *rifling grooves*. The bore diameter is only .30 inch.

Rifle Ammunition

Your choice of ammunition depends mainly on the size of the animal you hunt and the distance at which you do most of your shooting.

To determine the ammunition best-suited for the game you hunt, consult a *ballistics table*. Most ammunition catalogs contain ballistics information including bullet energy, muzzle velocity and the drop, all at different ranges.

A bullet's hitting power, or energy, is determined by its weight and velocity. The heavier and faster the bullet, the more energy it delivers to the target. At normal shooting ranges, a light, fast bullet generally delivers as much energy

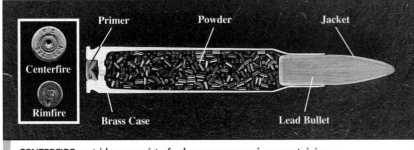

CENTERFIRE cartridges consist of a brass case; a primer containing a highly explosive compound that ignites when struck by the firing pin; powder, which is ignited by the priming compound; and a lead bullet, which may have a copper-zinc jacket to control the bullet's expansion. The inset shows spent centerfire and rimfire cases. With rimfires, the firing pin strikes the edge of the rim, igniting the priming compound.

and kills as effectively as a heavier but slower bullet. Hitting power is measured in *foot-pounds*.

Muzzle velocity or bullet speed is measured in feet per second. The faster the bullet is, for a given weight, the more energy it will carry. It will also fly flatter. The more powder the case holds the more velocity a bullet will have, when comparing bullets of the same size. The size of the brass case will affect how much powder will be behind the bullet.

The bullet's performance is affected by its size, weight and shape. The bullet's size, or diameter, is referred to as its *caliber.* This diameter corresponds to the diameter of the rifling in

BULLET STYLES include (1) pointed, streamlined for high velocity and flat trajectory. (2) Pointed boat tail *has a tapered base to reduce drag even more. (3)* Hollow points *mushroom rapidly, but no faster than (4)* flat and (5) round points, *often used in rifles with tubular magazines. Their blunt points will not detonate cartridges ahead of them, but result in relatively slow flight and short range. (6) Mushroomed bullet shows expansion.*

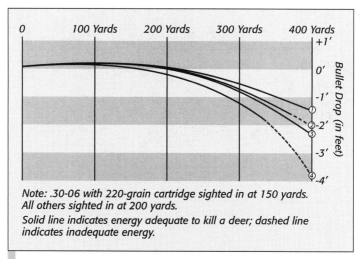

Note: .30-06 with 220-grain cartridge sighted in at 150 yards. All others sighted in at 200 yards.
Solid line indicates energy adequate to kill a deer; dashed line indicates inadequate energy.

LOAD affects trajectory and energy. This chart compares four .30 caliber bullets: (1) a 180-grain .300 Winchester Magnum and (2) 150-, (3) 180- and (4) 220-grain .30-06 bullets. The 180-grain .300 magnum has a flatter trajectory than the 180-grain .30-06. The 180-grain .30-06 retains energy longer but drops more than the 150-grain .30-06. The 220-grain .30-06 has the lowest velocity, so it drops most and has the shortest effective range.

the gun. Caliber is measured in decimal fractions of an inch; i.e., .300 or .30 is a 30 caliber. Some calibers are expressed in millimeters. The conversion to inches from millimeters is approximately .04. So a 7mm is approximately .280, 6mm a .240 and 7.5mm approximately a .300.

Bullet weight is measured in grains; a 150-grain bullet weighs almost exactly that much.

The shape of a bullet determines its friction or resistance in the air, affecting its *trajectory,* or flight path. A long, thin, streamlined pointed bullet will retain its velocity at longer ranges better than a short, stout bullet. So the longer bullet has a flatter trajectory. Trajectory is also affected by the bullet's velocity. A fast bullet flies flatter than a slow one.

The construction of a bullet also determines its ability to penetrate upon impact. The bullet should mushroom on impact and not break apart. Mushrooming transfers all the bullet's energy into the target.

Certain ammunition will shoot best in your rifle; each gun is a little different. Today's factory loads can perform up to the highest standards. Try different brands and loads till you find a particular cartridge that meets your needs and with which you can shoot tight groups.

TYPE OF CARTRIDGE	MUSCLE VELOCITY (in feet per second)	ENERGY (in foot-pounds) AND TRAJECTORY (in inches above (+) or below (−) line of aim)			
		100 Yards Energy/ Trajectory	200 Yards Energy/ Trajectory	300 Yards Energy/ Trajectory	400 Yards Energy/ Trajectory
.22 Long Rifle (40 Grain)	1255	92/0.0	−/−	−/−	−/−
.222 Remington (50 Grain)	3140	752/+2.2	500/+0.0	321/-10.0	202/-32.3
.243 Winchester (100 Grain)	2960	1615/+1.9	1332/0.0	1089/-7.8	882/-22.6
.270 Winchester (130 Grain)	3060	2225/+1.8	1818/0.0	1472/-7.4	1180/-21.6
7mm Rem. Magnum (150 Grain)	3110	2667/+1.7	2196/0.0	1792/-7.0	1448/-20.5
.30-30 Winchester (170 Grain)	2200	1355/+2.0	989/-4.8	720/-25.1	535/-63.6
.30-06 Springfield (150 Grain)	2910	2281/+2.1	1827/0.0	1445/-8.5	1131/-25.0
.300 Win. Magnum (180 Grain)	2960	3011/+1.9	2578/0.0	2196/-7.3	1859/-20.9
.375 H&H Magnum (270 Grain)	2690	3510/+2.5	2812/0.0	2228/-10.0	1747/-29.4

BALLISTICS TABLES help you determine the effective killing range of your cartridge and bullet drop at various ranges. This table lists muzzle velocity and the energy in foot-pounds delivered at ranges from 100 to 400 yards. As a rule, use a cartridge with at least 900 foot-pounds to kill a deer, 1500 for an elk and 2100 for a moose. Trajectory figures show how far the bullet strikes above (+) or below (-) the point of aim at ranges from 100 to 400 yards.

Never use ammunition other than that recommended for your rifle by the manufacturer. The result could be a damaged rifle and serious injury. The correct cartridge designation for your rifle will be stamped on the barrel next to the receiver, or chamber.

Sights

Even the best rifle is of little use without an accurate sighting device. Some hunters spend as much for a telescopic sight as for the rifle itself.

Many rifles come with iron sights. To aim, the hunter centers a post at the end of the barrel in a notch or peep-hole in the rear sight. Iron sights are inexpensive, lightweight, durable and best-suited for short-range shooting.

For more accurate, precise shooting or for shots at longer distances, hunters prefer telescopic sights, or *scopes*. A scope consists of a metal tube containing a system of lenses that magnify the target. The *reticle*, a network of lines or crosshairs inside the scope, enables you to aim precisely. The optics allow you to focus your eye on the reticle and target at the same time, so you can aim quickly. Scopes are not as durable as iron sights and are easier to knock out of adjustment.

Scopes vary in magnification power, from 1x, which magnifies the target 1 time, to 12x or more. Fixed power scopes have one magnification power. Variable power scopes allow you to change the magnification with the twist of an adjustment ring. Most hunters use scopes ranging in power from 2x to 9x. Low-power scopes work best for close-range shooting. They have a larger field of view, making it easy to find your target. Highpower scopes narrow the field of view, but help you see a distant animal.

A scope is attached to the gun using mounts or bases and rings. Whatever the mounting system, it must fit the scope, attach solidly to the gun and be adjusted to provide enough distance between the scope and your eye. Scopes should be at least 3 inches away from your eye, when the gun is shouldered, to allow for clearance when the gun recoils.

Most manufacturers offer a selection of special-purpose scopes designed specifically for shotguns and muzzleloaders.

TYPES OF SIGHTS AND SCOPES

•*4-Plex*™ reticles have wires that are thick toward the outside. These wires stand out against the background and draw your eye to the target. The thin crosshairs enable you to aim precisely, without obscuring the animal.

•*Open* sights have a blade or post, which must be centered in the notched rear sight. They are the most difficult of the sights to align, and the rear sight covers up part of the target.

•*Peep* sights require you to center the target in a hole in the rear sight, then place the bead directly on the animal. Hunters prefer large peep-holes so they can see most of the target.

•*Crosshair* reticles work best for long-range shooting. The fine wires provide a precise aiming point and cover little of the target. But the wires may be difficult to see in dim light.

•*Dot* reticles feature a small dot that keeps your eye on the center of the crosshairs. They work best for short-range shooting; at long ranges, the dot obscures much of the target.

•*Post* reticles have a thick post that stands out against dense timber or brush, and works well for tracking a moving target. At long range, the post may cover some of the target.

•*Wide-angle* scopes provide a wide field of view. Because you can see more terrain, you can spot animals more quickly. Wide-angle scopes enable you to follow running game.

HOW TO USE A VARIABLE POWER SCOPE

•*Turn* the adjustment ring on a variable power scope to change the magnification. Common power ranges are 1.5x to 4.5x, 2x to 7x, and 3x to 9x.

•*Keep* a variable scope on low power in most situations. At 3x power, for example, you can easily find and center a distant big-game animal in the scope.

•*Increase* the power for long-range shooting at standing game. At 9x, a distant big-game animal nearly fills the scope, making it easier to aim.

Sighting In Your Rifle

Many a hunter has lost his chance for a trophy because of a rifle that was not sighted in. Before hunting, sight in any new rifle or one that has been handled roughly.

You can sight in most easily at a shooting range. Most ranges have bench rests and sandbags to provide a steady rest and minimize human error. If sighting in your rifle in the field, make sure you shoot into a solid backstop.

To shoot accurately, take a deep breath, exhale halfway, then hold your breath as you squeeze the trigger. Do not jerk the trigger as you shoot.

Sights on a new rifle may be so far out of adjustment that

HOW TO ROUGH-SIGHT A RIFLE

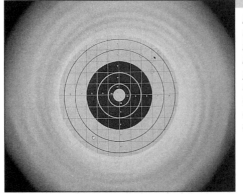

MOVE the rifle barrel until the center of the bore lines up with the bullseye of a target 25 yards away. Fix the rifle's position so it cannot move, then adjust the sights to aim at the bullseye.

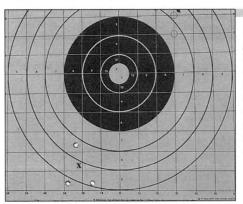

FIRE a three-shot group. The center of the group (X) is the average point of impact. If the center is not in the bullseye, adjust the sights. With a scope you should strive to get a group size of 1 inch wide at 100 yards.

you will miss the target completely. To solve this problem, *rough sight* your rifle at close range, generally about 25 yards. One method, termed *bore sighting,* involves sighting through the opening in the barrel. Look directly through the bore of the bolt or falling block action. You cannot look directly through the bore of most other actions, so you must use a bore-sighting tool.

SIGHT IN your rifle so the bullet hits just above the point of aim at 100 yards. For most flat-shooting cartridges, you should zero in 2 to 3 inches high; the exact distance depends on the trajectory of your bullet. By sighting in this way, you can aim dead-on at your target at any range up to 300 yards. The bullet will hit slightly high or low, depending on the range, but will strike somewhere in the animal's vital area.

You can also rough-sight your rifle by simply aiming at a close target through the sights, firing, then making any adjustments needed to hit the bullseye.

Once you have rough-sighted at 25 yards, back off to 100 yards. Continue to fine-tune the sights until you can center the shot group on the bullseye. If you plan to shoot at longer ranges, sight in a few inches high at 100 yards. Then try a few long-range shots and make any necessary adjustments.

Always hunt with the same type of ammunition you used to sight in. Changing brands or bullet weights often makes it necessary to realign your sights.

HOW TO ADJUST RIFLE SIGHTS

•*Adjust* iron sights by moving the rear sight in the direction you want the rifle to shoot. To make the rifle shoot higher, raise the rear sight. To make it shoot to the left, move the rear sight to the left.

•*Move* scope sights by turning elevation (up-down) and widage (right-left) screws the way you want the bullet impact to move. Read the instruction manual to see how much each click or mark changes the sight at 100 yards.

TIPS FOR SIGHTING IN YOUR RIFLE

•*Rest* the forearm and butt stock on sandbags when sighting in. Do not support the barrel; the result will be inaccurate shooting. Hold the stock firmly against your shoulder. Always wear eye and ear protection when on the range.

•*Carry* tools like small screwdrivers and hex keys to adjust sights and tighten mounts. Move adjuster screws on scopes with a coin.

•*Make* a bullseye with several 1-inch squares of black tape. The squares make it easy to judge the distance between a bullet hole and the bullseye.

•*Rest* the forearm of your rifle on a sandbag or folded jacket on your vehicle. Use a spotting scope to see bullet holes in the target.

Shooting a Rifle

Shooting a rifle under hunting conditions is more difficult than shooting at a target range. To shoot accurately, hunters must assume a stable position, and know how to compensate for wind, uphill or downhill angles and moving animals.

Whenever possible, try to find a stable object to provide a steady rest for your rifle. If you cannot find such an object, the prone position is your next best choice. But shooting from the prone position may be impossible if ground cover or rolling terrain obscures your line of sight. Under these conditions, most hunters use the sitting posi-

SOLID REST. If you shoot right-handed, rest your left hand or elbow on a solid object, like a tree or rock. Do not rest your rifle directly on the object.

PRONE. Lie with your body about 30 degrees left of your line of aim. Place your left elbow just left of the rifle. Pull your right leg forward to lift your stomach off the ground, so your breathing does not affect the shot.

tion, which offers good stability because both elbows rest on the knees. The kneeling position is less stable, because only one elbow rests on the knee. The offhand position is the least stable. However, it may be the only choice when a moving animal offers a brief chance for a shot.

Hunters should learn how to adjust for natural forces like *wind drift* and the *slant range effect*. A strong crosswind dramatically affects a bullet's flight path. To hit a standing target, you must compensate by aiming slightly upwind.

The slant range effect causes your bullet to hit high whenever you shoot uphill

SITTING. Sit with your legs about 30 degrees to the right of your line of aim and rest your elbows firmly on your knees. Sitting is the most useful shooting position. You can use the position almost anywhere, assume it quickly and shoot accurately.

KNEELING. Sit on your right foot with your body 45 degrees left of the line of aim. Place your left foot forward and your left elbow on the knee.

OFFHAND. Stand sideways with feet parallel to the line of aim. Spread your legs to shoulder width. Keep your left elbow close to your body.

or downhill. This confusing phenomenon results from the fact that gravity acts at a right angle to the horizontal. When a bullet is shot on a horizontal plane, gravity pulls at a right angle over the entire distance to the target, resulting in a curved flight path. But when a bullet is shot vertically, either straight up or straight down, gravity does not bend the flight path at all. The closer the angle to the vertical, the less the flight path curves.

A rifle is usually sighted in on the horizontal, so the sights are adjusted to compensate for maximum bullet drop. Since the bullet does not drop as much when shooting uphill or downhill, it always hits high. To compensate, aim low.

Most hunters tend to shoot behind running animals. A hunter using 150-grain .30-06 bullets would maintain a 4- to 5-foot lead at a deer running at a right angle 100 yards away. At 200 yards, he would increase the lead to about 10 feet and at 300 yards, to about 16 feet.

Practice your lead by shooting at a rolling tire with a cardboard target wedged inside. Position yourself on a hill, then have someone roll the tire past you.

FACTORS THAT AFFECT A BULLET'S FLIGHT PATH

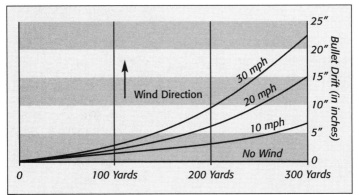

WIND DRIFT increases as wind velocity and range increase. The chart shows how crosswinds of 10, 20 and 30 mph would affect the path of a .30-06, 150-grain bullet at 100, 200 and 300 yards. As the chart indicates, a 10 mph crosswind would cause the bullet to drift less than 1 inch at 100 yards. But in a 30 mph crosswind, the bullet would drift over 22 inches at 300 yards.

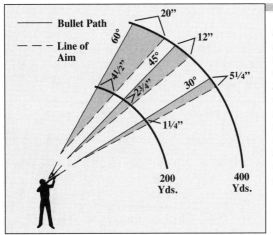

SLANT RANGE EFFECT increases with distance and angle. A 200-yard shot at 30 degrees hits about 1 inch higher than normal. A 400-yard shot at 60 degrees hits 20 inches higher.

Shotguns

Frontiersmen referred to the shotgun as a *scattergun* because it sprayed a swarm of lead pellets. A shot swarm is more effective than a single bullet for hitting moving targets.

When selecting a shotgun, consider the following: size of the bore; the *chokes* you will need, or the amount of barrel constriction; action; chamber length; weight; and barrel type.

BORE SIZE. Shotgun bores are measured in gauge or in inches. As gauge increases, the size of the bore decreases. The most common gauges are 12 and 20, but gauges range from as small as 28 to as large as 10. The smallest bore is the .410, the only bore measured in inches. The larger the bore, the more pellets a gun can shoot. The denser *shot pattern* increases the chances for a long-range kill.

CHOKE. The amount of constriction, or choke, at the end of the barrel affects the diameter and density of your shot pattern. Common chokes, from widest (most open) to narrowest (tightest), include cylinder, skeet, improved-cylinder, modified, improved-modified and full. Open chokes are best for close-range shooting; tight chokes, long-range. The improved-cylinder is a good all-around choice.

With a 12 gauge, improved cylinder choke and a standard-load No. 6 shell, about 13 pellets hit the vulnerable area of a stationary mallard silhouette at 40 yards. With a modified choke, about 16 pellets strike the target and with a full choke, about 20. Fewer pellets would strike a flying bird, because not all pellets in the shot swarm reach the target at the same time.

Many modern shotguns have interchangeable screw-in choke tubes that enable you to quickly change chokes to suit the type of hunting. A gunsmith can also install screw-in chokes in some older guns.

ACTION. Most single-shot and double-barreled shotguns have a *hinge* action. The action opens when you push a lever or button at the rear of the receiver, allowing you to manually insert the shells. After firing, you break the action again. If your gun has ejectors, the spent hulls pop out automatically; otherwise, you must remove them yourself. The simple hinge design is more reliable than repeating actions, like the pump and semi-automatic.

With a pump-action, the pump ejects the spent shell and chambers another one each time you slide the fore-end back and forth. The majority of pump-action shotguns hold 5 shells. Pump shotguns are more dependable than semi-automatics, which can malfunction in cold weather.

A semi-automatic fires one shell, ejects it and chambers another with each pull of the trigger. Most semi-automatics hold 5 shells, although a few hold up to 7.

CHAMBER LENGTH. Many shotguns are chambered for standard 2 3/4-inch shells. To shoot many types of magnum loads, you need a gun with a longer chamber. The proper shell length is usually engraved on the barrel. Never shoot a shell that exceeds that length.

WEIGHT. A light shotgun works best for quick shots in heavy cover. When you have more time to shoot, a heavier gun works better. You can hold the barrel steadier and swing on a target more smoothly.

BARREL TYPE. A long barrel gives you a long sighting plane and can improve your shooting accuracy. But contrary to popular belief, a longer barrel does not mean a noticeable increase in shooting range.

Many guns come with *ventilated ribs*. A rib makes it easier to sight down the barrel and cools it quickly, an advantage for rapid-fire shooting.

SHOTGUN TIPS

•*Proper fit* should be checked while wearing your hunting clothes. You should be able to bring the gun to your shoulder in one motion, without the butt catching on your clothing. When you point the gun, the heel of your thumb should be 2 to 3 inches from your nose.

•*Screw-in chokes* enable you to change your shot pattern for different types of hunting. Use a specially designed wrench to install and remove the chokes.

Shotgun Shells

Choosing shotgun shells is similar to selecting a rifle cartridge with one exception. You must use nontoxic shot for waterfowl. Next, consider the size of game you hunt and the distance you will normally shoot.

Size of the animal usually determines the size of shot. Hunters prefer small shot for small animals. It penetrates deep enough to kill, but does not damage too much meat. Larger shot would obviously kill a small animal, but the chances of missing it are greater. Shells with larger shot have fewer pellets, resulting in more open space in the pattern.

Large shot retains energy longer, so it carries farther and penetrates better than small shot. But very large shot is not necessarily better for long-range shooting. Use the largest shot that still has a sufficiently dense pattern at your usual shooting distance.

Load, or weight of the shot and strength of the powder charge, will also affect your shooting range. *Field* loads have the least shot and weakest powder charge with increasing charges in *standard* and *magnum* loads. For example, 12 gauge, 2³/4-inch shells come in field loads that contain 1¹/8 ounces of shot and 3¹/4 dram equivalents of powder; standard loads with 1¹/4 ounces of shot and 3³/4 dr. equivs. of powder; and magnum loads with 1¹/2 ounces of shot and 3³/4 dr. equivs. of powder.

SHOT SHELL PARTS include: (1) hull, the outer shell usually made of plastic or paper with a metal base; (2) shot, round lead or nontoxic pellets; (3) powder, which is ignited by (4) primer when firing pin strikes it; (5) wad, a plastic or fiber divider that separates powder and shot.

Field loads are adequate for close-range shooting at squirrels and rabbits, and for small to medium-sized birds. Standard loads work better at longer ranges, and for larger animals. Many hunters believe that magnum loads greatly increase their shooting range. But a magnum of the same length as a standard load may actually have a slightly lower velocity and a shorter range. The advantage of a magnum is a denser shot pattern.

Shot pattern depends on pellet size and the choke of your barrel. For example, with a modified choke and a standard 12 gauge shell and No. 6 shot, about 34 pellets strike the vulnerable area of a stationary mallard silhouette at 30 yards, about 16 pellets at 40 yards, and 12 at 50 yards. With No. 2 shot and the same choke, about 13 pellets hit the mallard target at 30 yards, about 5 at 40 yards, and 2 at 50 yards.

Some magnum shells have longer cases that hold even more shot and powder. A 12 gauge, 3-inch magnum, for example, contains 1⅞ ounces of shot and 4 dr. equivs. of powder. Its effective range is about 10 yards longer than a standard 2¾-inch load. Never attempt to shoot a long cased magnum shell in a gun chambered for standard shells.

Most often used for big-game hunting, slug loads are available in two basic styles: sabot-type and Foster-style. While slugs are available for almost all gauges, 12 gauge slugs are the most popular.

POPULAR SLUGS include: (1) sabot-type, with a plastic sleeve (the sabot) that encases an elongated projectile. Sabots are very accurate and ballistically superior to (2) Foster-style slugs, which have a cup-shaped, nose-heavy design.

RECOMMENDED SHOT SIZES

Cottontail Rabbits	6-7½	Dove	6-8
Squirrels	5-7½	Woodcock	7½-9
Ring-Necked Pheasants	4-6	Small Ducks	1-5
Grouse	6-8	Large Ducks	BB-3
Turkey	4-6	Large Geese	T-BB

Shooting a Shotgun

Expert shotgunners develop their skills through practice. It takes little skill to hit a standing target with a shotgun, but moving game is a challenge. You must adjust for different angles, ranges and flight speeds, all within seconds.

Because a moving animal offers only a brief opportunity for a shot, you must learn to mount the gun quickly and consistently. Place the butt against your shoulder and press your cheek against the stock. Keep both eyes open and sight down the barrel with your dominant eye, which for most right-handed shooters is the right eye.

Practice mounting the gun and operating the safety at home. Wear your hunting coat, and make sure that you can bring the gun to your shoulder without it catching on your clothing. Quickly draw a bead on stationary objetcs. Rotate your shoulders and hips as if following a moving target. Be sure your shotgun is unloaded before you practice.

Shotgunners use three basic techniques for moving game. *Snap-shooting* works well at close range. But for crossing targets at longer distances, use the *swing-through* or *sustained-lead* methods.

To sharpen your accuracy, shoot at practice targets, or *clay pigeons*. Practice at a shooting range or have a friend throw clay pigeons with a *hand trap*. Fire at crossing, overhead and straight-away targets, so you learn how to shoot at different angles.

THE SWING-THROUGH TECHNIQUE

START your swing with the barrel behind the bird. Move the barrel smoothly and steadily, so it starts to catch up with the bird's tail.

CONTINUE swinging so the barrel moves ahead of the bird. How far ahead depends on the distance and the speed and angle of the bird's flight.

PULL the trigger when you think you have reached the proper lead. Do not hesitate, flinch or slow down your swing as you pull the trigger.

FOLLOW THROUGH until the barrel is well past the bird. If you stop swinging too soon, you will shoot behind the target.

THE SNAP-SHOOTING TECHNIQUE

SNAP-SHOOTING is the most effective technique for quick shots at crossing or straight-away targets at close range in heavy cover.

POINT your barrel at the spot where you think the bird will be when the shot arrives, and pull the trigger.

WATCH closely for the spot where the bird falls; in heavy cover, downed birds are often difficult to find.

THE SUSTAINED-LEAD TECHNIQUE

SUSTAINED-LEAD shooting works well when a long-range target offers ample time to aim. Determine your lead, hold the barrel that far ahead of the bird, and pull the trigger while maintaining your lead.

HOW TO ESTIMATE SHOOTING RANGE

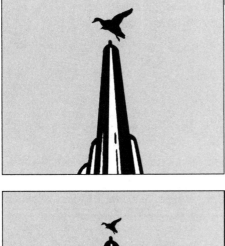

COMPARE the head-to-tail length of a crossing bird to the muzzle width of your shotgun. At 20 yards (top), a mallard duck appears nearly twice as long as the width of a 12 gauge shotgun's muzzle. At 45 yards (bottom), the bird's length is about the same as the width of the muzzle. A large Canada goose is almost twice as long as the muzzle at 30 yards; slightly longer at 45 yards; and approximately the same length at 60 yards.

Bowhunting

Bowhunting is one of the more difficult and rewarding forms of hunting. It takes more dedication and practice to become proficient with this primitive weapon. In most cases the hunter needs to get much closer than the hunter using a gun. So the bowhunter needs to refine his hunting skills as well as his shooting skills.

Bowhunting is very popular for many reasons: hunters using a bow are generally allowed longer hunting seasons; this form of hunting is a big challenge; it is a very relaxing and peaceful form of hunting; and it is fun.

There are basically three types of bows: the compound bow, the recurve and the longbow (opposite page). Your choice of bow type is largely a matter of personal preference, each having its advantages and disadvantages.

The most popular hunting bow is the *compound,* which uses cams and cables to give the bow *let-off,* a reduction in the amount of force needed to hold the bow at full draw. This is an advantage when holding the bow back while waiting for a shot opportunity.

The peak *draw weight,* or maximum amount of weight needed to draw the bow, can be adjusted on a compound bow, whereas on a longbow or recurve, the draw weight is determined by the design of the bow. For a given draw weight a compound bow will produce more energy than a recurve or longbow. Determining your proper draw weight starts by trying different bows. Select a bow with a draw weight that you can draw very comfortably. One of the biggest problems bowhunters have is trying to hunt with bows that have excessive draw weight.

In general, many bows with a 60-pound draw weight are

EQUIPMENT FOR BOWHUNTING

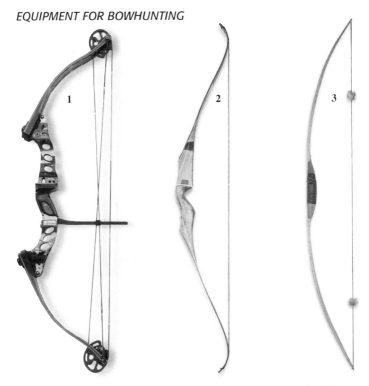

BOWS INCLUDE: (1) compound bows, (2) recurve bows, (3) longbows. Compounds deliver the most energy for a given draw weight; longbows the least. A compound's limbs are made of man-made materials. Recurves and longbows are usually made of fiberglass-wood laminates, though some longbows are solid wood.

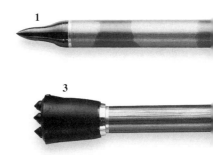

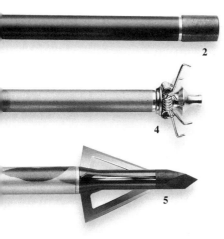

ARROWHEADS INCLUDE: (1) field points for practice, (2) steel blunts, (3) rubber blunts, (4) JUDO® points for small game and field practice, and (5) broadheads for hunting larger game.

heavy enough for all North American game animals. In truth, it is the *kinetic energy* – not a bow's poundage, – that matters most. Kinetic energy is a measurement based on the speed and weight of the arrow used. The higher the kinetic energy of an arrow, the more penetrating power or killing ability the arrow will have.

Kinetic energy is also affected by your own *draw length*. This is the distance between the bowstring and the grip when you hold a bow at full draw. Do not confuse draw length with arrow length; arrows are often shorter or longer than your draw length. For a given bow type, a longer draw length will produce more energy than a short draw length.

The design of the *cams* or wheels on compound bows will also affect the bow's ability to produce energy. The rounder the cams – or on one-cam bows, the cam – the less arrow speed the bow will be able to produce. However, they are easier to draw, more forgiving to shoot and quieter. Radical cams produce faster arrow speed, flatter trajectory and more energy, but they are also harder to shoot, noisier and more difficult to maintain.

Arrow weight also affects the amount of energy that you can deliver into a target. A heavier arrow will produce more energy. However, an arrow that is too heavy for a particular bow will not perform well. Consult an arrow selection chart or archery shop to help you choose the correct shaft.

Some hunters prefer to hunt with recurve and longbows. They are lighter, quieter to shoot and less prone to mechanical failure. These more traditional bows increase the challenge and add nostalgia to the hunt.

Shooting a Bow and Arrow

In the hands of an experienced shooter, the bow and arrow can be very accurate. But the average hunter stands little chance of killing an animal with a bow, unless he is willing to take the time to practice.

Shooting a bow and arrow accurately is more difficult than shooting a firearm. You must build up the muscles you use to shoot, use the correct shooting mechanics and be able to concentrate. You also need to practice and develop your ability to judge distances accurately.

The first key to good shooting is the ability to relax. Learn to let the bow shoot the arrow. If you try to force the arrow into the target you will not shoot consistently.

A good stance is very important in shooting accurately. If your upper body moves around, your sights and bow will be moving, too. It is your legs that hold it all still.

CORRECT SHOOTING FORM requires proper body position, a good stance and correct hand positions.

Begin by standing with your feet spread apart at shoulder width, 90 degrees to the target. Then take a half-step back with the front foot and pivot slightly toward the target for a mildly open stance. Keep your weight evenly distributed on both feet, and stand straight up, with your head directly over the center of your body. Maintain this stance as you raise the bow to shoot. Don't lean forward or backward to pull the bow, and don't cock your head to the side to line up your sights. In some cases, you will not be able to shoot standing straight up, but try to position yourself in a way that gives you good upper body stability.

Your string hand, like the bow hand, should stay relaxed thoughout the drawing process. There are two basic styles that hunters use to hold and release bowstrings. The more traditional method is to use your fingers. If you release with

TYPICAL ANCHOR POINTS

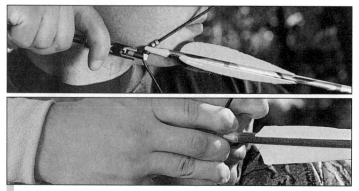

USING a wrist-strap release aid, many archers anchor with the big knuckle behind the jaw (top). With a finger-held release, most archers anchor so the tip of the index or middle finger is at the corner of the mouth.

your fingers, start by grasping the string at the first joints of your first three fingers, with the index finger above the nock, the other two fingers below the nock. As you draw, the middle finger should hold most of the weight, and the other two fingers should float on the string. The other method for releasing the bow involves using a mechanical release aid. Choose one that has a rotating head, so it will not torque the string as you draw. With a wrist-strap release, you should pull only on the strap, and your fingers should remain loose. With a finger-held release, your wrist should stay straight and relaxed.

When you draw a bow, hold it at arm's length, roughly aiming at the target, and begin to draw, pulling only with the muscles of your back. When you reach full draw, anchor solidly and aim at the target.

The anchor point for finger shooters is typically fairly high, with the tip of the index or middle finger planted solidly in the corner of the mouth. There is not necessarily a best way to anchor when using a release aid. With a wrist-strap release, many hunters anchor with the big knuckle of the index finger pressed behind the jaw. With a finger-held release aid, experienced shooters commonly anchor with the back of the hand pressed against the jaw.

No matter what type of equipment you use or the release

method you use, the release should happen through complete relaxation. Focus your attention on pulling the bowstring with your back muscles. Release shooters will be pulling the release trigger as their back muscles tighten up; finger shooters should let the string slip away as their hand relaxes. The shot should happen as a surprise.

Follow through a shot by holding your bow arm and release hand in the same position they were in when you released, till the arrow hits the target.

Always practice from the positions in which you hunt. If you use a tree stand, practice from an elevated platform. If you sit in your stand, practice in the sitting position. Wear your hunting clothes when practicing; they may affect your shooting. Use an arm guard to prevent the string from catching on heavy clothes.

"Stump-shooting" may be the most valuable practice of all. Whenever possible, roam through the woods and fields and shoot at rotten stumps, dirt clods and grass clumps with a Judo point.

BOW CARE TIPS

•*Inspect* the bowstring before shooting; frayed strings should be replaced.

•*Lubricate* your bowstring regularly with beeswax or a commercial bowstring wax.

•*Keep* your bow away from heat. Laminated bow limbs can come apart after only a few hours in a hot vehicle.

Muzzleloaders

Hunters who accept the challenge of making one shot count can gain the benefit of additional seasons when they start hunting with a muzzleloader. Most states have special muzzleloader regulations that extend big-game

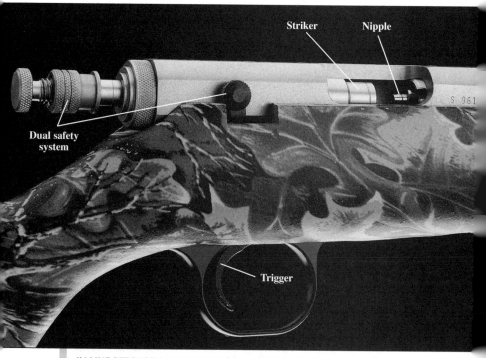

IN-LINE PERCUSSION CAPLOCKS have an internal striker or hammer that is cocked by pulling it rearward. When the trigger is pulled, the striker slams forward and hits the percussion cap, which is positioned on a nipple. The nipple is positioned directly behind the powder charge, so the fire from the cap reaches it instantly.

hunting opportunities beyond normal gun seasons. Muzzle-loaders or black powder guns must be loaded by inserting powder and bullet or shot into the muzzle, then pressing the load down the barrel toward the breech. Reloading after a shot can take a minute or more in most cases, requiring the first shot to be a good one.

Hunters have a choice between muzzleloading shotguns and rifles. Each one of these is available in different ignition systems. The three most popular with hunters include in-line percussion caplock, percussion caplock and flintlock. Flintlock, the oldest ignition system, has never been very reliable for the hunter. The percussion caplock, developed in 1820, increased the muzzleloader's reliability. It wasn't until the mid-1980s that the first in-line muzzleloaders

OTHER COMMON IGNITION SYSTEMS

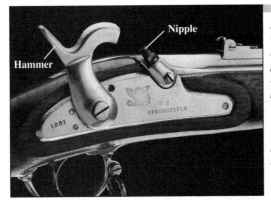

PERCUSSION CAPLOCK. The hammer strikes a percussion cap, similar to the primer of a modern cartridge. A flash travels through the nipple to ignite the powder charge.

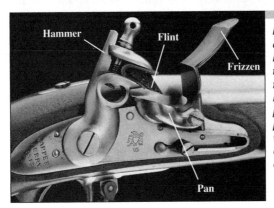

FLINTLOCKS have a flint in the hammer. When the flint strikes a frizzen, sparks ignite the primer powder. Flame passes through a vent hole to set off the powder charge.

PROJECTILES

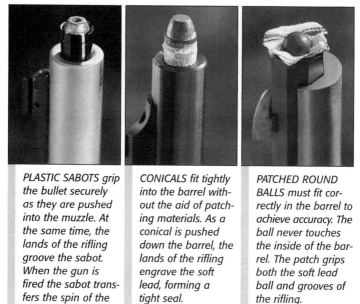

PLASTIC SABOTS grip the bullet securely as they are pushed into the muzzle. At the same time, the lands of the rifling groove the sabot. When the gun is fired the sabot transfers the spin of the rifling to the bullet.

CONICALS fit tightly into the barrel without the aid of patching materials. As a conical is pushed down the barrel, the lands of the rifling engrave the soft lead, forming a tight seal.

PATCHED ROUND BALLS must fit correctly in the barrel to achieve accuracy. The ball never touches the inside of the barrel. The patch grips both the soft lead ball and grooves of the rifling.

were developed. These frontloaders became a very reliable hunting weapon. The in-line design allows the percussion cap to be located very close to the powder charge, promoting quicker and more positive ignition.

The most popular muzzleloading rifles for big game are .50 or .54 caliber. The projectile may be a patched round ball, a conical or a saboted bullet. An in-line rifle firing a saboted bullet can achieve good accuracy at 100 yards, comparable to modern centerfires, and have a killing range on whitetail-size animals out to 150 yards. The practical accuracy range of a patched round ball is approximately 80 yards; a conical, 100 yards. A modern in-line muzzleloader properly loaded with a heavy, well-constructed bullet is up to the task of downing any North American game animal.

A hunter today has a choice of types of powder to use in his gun. He can use the centuries-old black powder or a synthetic black powder called Pyrodex™. Either type will perform well, and the hunter can test to see which one performs best in his gun.

The use of muzzleloading shotguns is not widespread, but these guns work well on waterfowl, upland game birds and turkeys. Small caliber muzzleloading rifles are used for small game and varmint hunting. Be sure to check the regulations in the area you plan to hunt when using these muzzleloaders.

BULLET TRAJECTORY

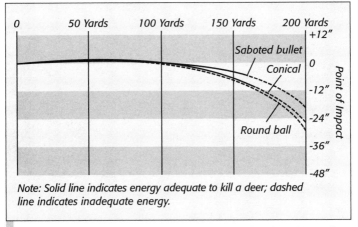

Note: Solid line indicates energy adequate to kill a deer; dashed line indicates inadequate energy.

BULLET TRAJECTORY for saboted bullets is flatter that that of conicals and round balls. As the chart above shows, a saboted bullet sighted in at 100 yards hits only 1½ inches high at 50 yards and 6 inches low at 150 yards.

Hunting Safety

ESTABLISH safe firing zones when hunting with others. When driving game, hunters should shoot only within the zones indicated by arrows.

Most people would be surprised to learn that hunting is one of the safest sports. A National Safety Council study showed the fatality rate for hunting to be less than half that of boating or swimming.

Improved hunter education and increased use of fluorescent orange clothing account for the low accident rate. Every state and province sponsors some type of firearms safety or hunter education program. Many states require beginning hunters to pass such a course before they can purchase a license.

Nevertheless, the potential for a serious accident always exists. To avoid an accident, follow these safety rules.

•*Treat* every firearm as if it is loaded. Never assume a gun is unloaded because someone said so.

•*Never* point a weapon at anything you do not mean to shoot. This includes glassing other hunters with your rifle scope.

•*Keep* the safety on and your finger away from the trigger until you are ready to shoot. This eliminates the possibility of discharging the gun accidentally, especially if you stumble or fall.

•*Positively* identify your target before shooting. Never fire at a silhouette, a vague form or an area where you saw or heard something move. Fluorescent orange clothing will greatly improve your own visibility.

•*Control* the direction of your muzzle at all times. If you start to fall, point the barrel away from yourself and other hunters. After a fall, check the barrel for obstructions like dirt or snow. A plugged barrel could rupture when you shoot, possibly causing serious injury.

•*Never* lean a gun against a tree, fencepost, vehicle or any place where it could fall over and accidentally discharge.

•*Never* shoot at hard surfaces or water with bullets or slugs. They could ricochet and strike another hunter or a building.

•*Use* only the ammunition recommended for your firearm. Do not carry two different types of ammunition in your pocket at the same time.

•*Never shoot* if there is a chance of hitting buildings, livestock or any other unintended target. Avoid shooting over the tops of hills and ridges.

•*Open* your action before crossing a creek or climbing over a fence, or in any other situation where you are unsure of your footing.

•*Position* your duck boat sideways to the shooting area. Do not position the boat lengthwise; this places one hunter in the other's shooting zone.

•*Split* the area around your waterfowl blind into 180-degree shooting zones. Each hunter scans for birds in the semicircle around his half of the blind.

•*When* not hunting, keep the gun unloaded and the action open.

•*Never* drink alcoholic beverages before or during a hunt. Alcohol will not keep you warm; instead, it speeds the loss of body heat.

•*Keep* all firearms and ammunition out of the reach of children.

•*Refuse* to hunt with anyone who does not observe the basic rules of firearms safety.

3

HUNTING

STRATEGIES

Planning Your Hunt

Advance planning is the key to a good hunting trip. Whether you travel to another state or hunt around home, lay the groundwork for your trip early.

Preparations for an out-of-state hunt should begin a year ahead. Some states conduct drawings for non-resident permits to hunt animals like elk, deer, pronghorn or wild turkey. Most states accept applications until spring, but some set deadlines as early as mid-winter.

Begin planning your trip by requesting non-resident hunting information from the wildlife agency in the state or province where you plan to hunt. Be sure to specify the type of game you will be hunting. Ask about drawing application deadlines and information on state and federal wildlife areas that may require advance reservations. Licenses may be offered on a first-come, first-served basis. Some states require hunters to show evidence of having passed a firearms safety or hunter education course.

Reservations and permits may also be necessary when hunting in your own state. Wildlife managers and conservation officers can provide information on special hunts that require advance preparation. They can also supply current game census data to help you choose a hunting area. Managers may know of local farmers or ranchers who want hunters to thin over-abundant game populations.

Many hunters join sportsmen's clubs, where they can share information on local game populations and habitat conditions. Some clubs lease private land where members can hunt.

Late summer is the best time to contact private landowners. Some farmers and ranchers tire of frequent interruptions during the hunting season. Once you get to know a landowner, you can phone ahead for permission to hunt rather than disturb him in early morning or interrupt his work.

TIPS ON PLANNING A HUNT

•*Always ask* for permission to hunt on private land. Introduce yourself and specify the type of game you wish to hunt. Some landowners will grant permission to a courteous hunter, even though their land is posted.

•*Talk* to a clerk at a sporting goods store for local hunting information. Many stores employ knowledgeable hunters. Most carry maps, permit applications and other items for planning your hunt.

•*Gather* information from state and federal wildlife agencies. They supply maps, brochures on public hunting areas, public access lists, and regulations. Tourist bureaus can recommend motels, resorts and campgrounds.

•*County maps* identify paved and unpaved roads. They also show section lines, buildings, public lands, lakes and streams. Plat books detail property lines and identify landowners. Maps and plat books are usually available at county offices.

•*Aerial photographs* reveal important details lacking on maps. They show isolated ponds and marshes, small streams, vegetation types, logging areas, meadows and forest trails. They can be obtained from the U.S. Department of Agriculture and private survey firms.

•*Topographic maps,* like U.S. Forest Service maps and U.S. Geological Survey maps, provide information on land elevation and detail other features of the landscape, such as wetlands. They also show buildings, roads, trails, portages and other features useful for finding your way on a hunting trip. Geological Survey maps show forested areas in green. They generally cover a larger area than Forest Service maps.

Scouting for Game

Pre-season scouting will improve your odds of finding game once the hunting season begins. Scouting is enjoyable in itself and saves valuable hunting time later.

Scouting enables you to become familiar with the terrain and to identify heavily-used game trails. It also helps you to determine any changes in habitat conditions or fluctuations in game populations that could affect your hunting.

Severe winter storms, wildlife food shortages, drought and cold or wet weather during nesting can drastically reduce game populations. New roads, housing developments and wetland drainage can permanently eliminate good wildlife habitat. So there is no guarantee that last year's prime hunting spot will produce game this year.

Binoculars and spotting scopes will help you find game from a distant vantage point. But even if you do not see animals, you can detect their presence by the signs they leave. Squirrels build nests in trees and scatter nut shells on the ground. Waterfowl preen themselves and leave feathers around resting areas. Bull elk bugle and roll in wallows during the mating period. All animals can be identified from their tracks and droppings.

Glass a potential hunting area from a nearby hill or tree. Look closely at edges between openings and cover to detect movement. You are most likely to see game early in the morning, at dusk or on cloudy days. When you spot an animal, note the time and identify a landmark to pinpoint the exact location. If the animal is not disturbed, it may appear in the same area at about the same time on subsequent days.

SIGNS OF GAME ACTIVITY

•*Tracks* in damp soil may reveal how long ago an animal passed. Fresh tracks have sharp edges. Older tracks have fuzzy edges. In snow, old tracks have a hard crust.

•*Droppings* help hunters find game. Large quantities indicate feeding, loafing or bedding areas. Some animals do not digest their food completely, so you can check droppings to determine what they have been eating.

•*Feeding signs* include damaged crops; scratched earth; nipped ends on grasses or twigs; and pits, husks and shells of fruits or nuts. Experienced hunters can often identify an animal by these signs.

•*Damaged trees and brush* result from animals rubbing with their antlers, scratching trees to mark their territory, or chewing bark. Each species has distinctive rubs, scrapes and chews.

•*Beds and roosts* in tall grass or on soft earth reveal the resting spots of mammals and birds. You can identify the animal from the size of its bed or roost and from nearby droppings, hair or feathers.

•*Game trails* lead from cover to food or water. Several kinds of game often use the same trail. Inspect it closely and look for fresh tracks made by the animals you will be hunting.

Still-Hunting

A still-hunter must pit his senses against those of his quarry. The term *still*, used this way, means silent, not motionless.

When still-hunting, always move slowly, keeping alert for sounds, visual signs and even odors that reveal the presence of game. When you move slowly, it is easier to see and hear animals, but more difficult for them to detect you.

Still-hunting works best when game is not active. Many hunters prefer to stand-hunt (page 64) in early morning, still-hunt during midday, then return to their stands in late afternoon.

The typical strategy is to walk at an extremely slow pace, taking only a few steps at a time. Stop, then wait for at least as long as you walked, slowly moving only your head and eyes. The length of each walking and waiting period varies, depending on the type of animal you are hunting. The periods are generally short for small game, but up to 5 minutes or longer for big game.

Whenever possible, walk into the wind so animals cannot detect your scent. Place each footstep carefully to prevent snapping twigs, crunching leaves or brushing against branches. Avoid crossing open areas and places where animals could see your form above the horizon. Try to stay near cover where game will not notice your movements.

The still-hunter does not know the exact location of an animal. Instead, he moves through likely-looking cover in hopes of surprising game. Expert hunters may get so close that animals burst from cover near their feet.

Still-hunting is usually a one-hunter method, but it also works well with two. Game surprised by one person may run toward the other. Or an animal may be so intent on watching one hunter that it does not detect another approaching.

Successful still-hunting demands patience and confidence. If you lose patience and begin moving too fast, animals will spook. If you are confident of seeing game, it is easier to stay alert.

TIPS FOR STILL-HUNTING

•*Wear* soft clothing to reduce noise. Hard-finish materials like nylon make swishing sounds as they brush the cover. Gummy bootsoles enable you to walk quietly.

•*Detect* wind direction and rising and falling thermals by squeezing unscented powder into the air or by tossing a small amount of down into the air.

•*Look* for visual clues to find game. A horizontal line among trees could be an animal's back. A glinting eye or twitching ear could also reveal game.

•*Avoid* walking or waiting in direct sunlight. Animals are quick to notice the glare off your face and clothing. They are less likely to see a hunter in the shade.

Stand-Hunting

The secret to successful stand-hunting is to position yourself where you are likely to see game, but game is not likely to see you. The technique works best early or late in the day, when animals move between resting and feeding areas.

Hunters conceal themselves on *stands* or in *blinds*. A stand may be nothing more than a large tree that obscures your form. Or it may be an elevated platform, either free-standing or attached to a tree trunk or limb. A blind provides more cover. Many have walls of camouflage material or vegetation.

Whether hunting from a blind or stand, choose a spot where game is likely to pass. Scout the area to find heavily-used game trails or flight paths. Take your position and get ready well before game begins moving. You may have to find your spot in the dark.

The wind can play a major role in choosing your site. When hunting big game, take a stand downwind of the area where you expect to see animals. Select alternative locations for different wind conditions. To insure that animals will not detect human scent, many hunters use odor eliminating products or masking scents. The sight and smell of smoke will alert game.

Wind direction is also important when hunting ducks or geese on water. Choose a blind on the lee side of natural cover. Waterfowl usually land into the wind in the calmer water.

Stand-hunters sometimes wear camouflage outfits to reduce their visibility. But many types of hunting require high-visibility clothing for safety purposes. Even if you wear fluorescent orange clothing, game will be less likely to see you if you keep motion to a minimum. If you must move, do so very slowly. Keep your face hidden; look at game from the side of your eye or from behind a hat brim.

Comfort is important when stand-hunting. You cannot remain quiet and motionless if you are cold, wet or in an uncomfortable position. You need warm clothing, because you must remain stationary for long periods. Some hunters build roofs to shed rain, or use padded seats and stoves. Waterfowl hunters sometimes build blinds that are completely enclosed except for shooting windows.

HOW TO SELECT A STAND-HUNTING LOCATION

•*Locate* your stand or blind near a watering site or stream crossing. Dove and antelope hunters often hunt near water holes. Moose hunters carefully check streambanks for heavily-used trails leading to water.

•*Choose* a site near a feeding area. Goose hunters build blinds or dig pits in harvested fields. Deer hunters take stands along the edges of corn, hay or milo fields. Bear hunters sometimes bait an area, then hunt nearby.

•*Select* a stand site in a location where you are not silhouetted against the skyline. Game will detect your movement more easily if you do not have a backdrop.

•*Avoid* stands that do not offer a clear field of fire. A tree or branch too close to your stand will narrow your shooting zone. A stand that restricts hip movement makes it difficult to swing your gun.

Stalking

L ike still-hunting, stalking demands fine-tuned hunting skills, because you must slip up on game without being detected. Stalking differs from still-hunting in that you know the location of the animal. Sneaking within shooting range can be extremely difficult, but expert stalkers often approach within a few feet of game.

Many stalkers use binoculars or spotting scopes. Because you can see an animal from farther away, it is less likely to detect you before you can adequately plan your strategy. When you spot an animal, watch it closely for a few min-

utes to determine whether it is likely to remain in the same area long enough for a stalk. If the animal is moving or appears nervous, you will probably not be able to get close enough for a shot. If it is feeding or bedded down, your odds are much better.

Stalking works best where the topography or cover will conceal your approach. Before beginning your stalk, plot a course that takes you into the wind, but keeps you behind hills, trees, brush, fencelines or other natural or man-made features.

If there is no cover, use a clump of vegetation to break up your outline. Camouflage clothing will also make you less visible. Move only when the animal faces away from you or when its head is down. Be sure that sunlight does not reflect off your gun or scope. If the animal sees you, walk away until you are out of sight. It may resume what it was doing, giving you another opportunity.

Move silently during the final stages of the stalk. Noise may not be important if you shoot from 300 yards. But for the bowhunter who must approach within 30 yards, any noise can ruin his chances.

It is usually best to stay concealed until after the shot. But waterfowl hunters sometimes rush the birds before they shoot. They may gain an extra 5 to 10 yards before the birds take off.

HOW TO STALK GAME

•*Pinpoint* game by identifying nearby landmarks like a tree, boulder or fencepost. You can stay hidden while using the landmark to guide your approach.

•*Plan* your stalk so you move directly into or quarter into the wind. This prevents the wind from carrying your scent and the sound of your approach to the animal.

•*Use* natural cover to conceal your approach. A fenceline, a drainage ditch or a field of tall crops or grass will enable you to sneak within gun range.

•*Bring* your own cover when hunting in flat, open country. Push a clump of weeds ahead of you, and stay low so game cannot spot your form above the horizon.

Driving

Alone hunter has little chance of rousting game from a large expanse of cover. Most animals sit tight or move off to the side rather than run or fly.

Driving is an effective way to push game out of cover. You can make a drive with anywhere from two to over a dozen hunters, depending on the situation. Before the drive begins, *posters* sneak to positions at the end of cover, where they intercept game pushed to them by *drivers*. The drivers spread out across the field or woods. The denser the vegetation, the closer they must be to discourage game from doubling back between them. It is generally better to have more drivers than posters.

Drives work best in a corridor or block of cover surrounded by open land. Game will usually stay in the cover until pushed to the end, assuring someone of a shot. If possible, start at the widest end and work toward the narrowest. This concentrates the animals in a relatively small area, increasing your chances of a close shot.

Hunters should always know the position of other drivers and posters. Wear fluorescent orange clothing for maximum visibility and never shoot in the direction of another hunter.

DRIVERS should stay within sight of each other. Outside drivers often move ahead to prevent game from escaping out the sides. Be especially alert as drivers approach posters; cornered game may spring from cover.

WHERE TO CONDUCT A DRIVE

•*Islands* of cover are ideal for drives. A patch of high brush in an open field, a shelterbelt or a woodlot is likely to hold game. If you attempt to hunt these areas alone, game may escape out the opposite side.

•*Corridors* of cover, like roadside ditches, canyons, stream courses and railroad tracks, make good places for a drive. Game is less likely to double back in a narrow strip of cover than in a wide expanse.

Flushing

For many types of game, the surest way to evade hunters is to hide in dense cover. Even animals as large as a deer or as brightly colored as a rooster pheasant can hide within a few feet of hunters without being noticed.

Hunters who use dogs stand the best chance of flushing tight-holding animals. Even in thick brush or other dense cover, a good dog will detect and follow an animal's scent. Without a dog, you are sure to walk by some game.

A lone hunter can unnerve animals, causing them to flush. Unusual sounds and erratic movements may cause game to become nervous and burst from cover. Many hunters yell, clap their hands, crack brush or even blow whistles as they walk. By varying your walking speed, stopping, turning back suddenly, or even running a few steps, you may convince an animal that it has been discovered.

STOP frequently when attempting to flush game. If you walk at a steady pace, animals usually sit tight because they are confident they have not been detected. When you stop, they lose confidence and attempt to escape.

When hunting with a partner, try to flush game toward each other. Start at opposite ends of the cover and attempt to trap game in the middle. This cuts off possible escape routes. And because the animal detects danger from two directions, it is more likely to flush.

TIPS FOR FLUSHING GAME

•*Throw* sticks or rocks to flush game from dense brush piles or other cover too thick to walk through. Game will usually attempt to slip out the opposite side, so watch carefully and be ready for a shot.

•*Kick* or step on clumps of vegetation that could hold birds or small game. With a hunter this close, game may be reluctant to flush. Tracks, droppings, feathers or hair may reveal the animal's presence.

Hunting Dogs

One of the hunter's most valuable assets is a well-trained hunting dog. Watching a good dog in action adds to the thrill of the hunt. And a dog with flushing, pointing or retrieving skills will greatly improve your hunting success.

Before selecting a dog, consider the type of game you intend to hunt, the terrain and climate. Pointing and flushing breeds were originally developed for hunting upland birds, most retrievers for waterfowl, and most hounds for small game. Many breeds work well for more than one type of game. The Labrador, for example, is an excellent waterfowl retriever, but is also favored by many upland bird hunters for its flushing skills.

When hunting upland birds in a large expanse of light cover, use a dog that ranges widely. Pointing breeds work beyond gun range. When they detect a strong scent, they freeze in position, or *point*. This gives the hunter time to walk in and flush the bird. For finding birds in thicker cover, a flushing dog may work better. These dogs work the cover slowly and thoroughly, usually staying within gun range.

Thorny cover can penetrate the fur and cut a short-haired dog. Long-haired breeds can tolerate thorns, but their fur often becomes matted with burrs.

In cold weather, a heavy-coated breed retains body heat longer than a dog with a thin coat. A thick coat is especially important for a dog that must retrieve in icy water. In extremely hot weather, a thin-coated breed works best. A dog with thick fur would overheat quickly.

A hunter must learn to *read* his dog, because every dog behaves somewhat differently when it smells game. With a pointing dog, a loose point usually means that the game has slipped away. A staunch point generally means game is close. Retrieving and flushing breeds perk up their ears or wag their tails rapidly. Hounds bay when they detect game.

Proper training and conditioning are the keys to developing a good dog. A poorly-trained dog is worse than no dog at

all. If it does not obey basic commands, it may flush game out of range. Or the dog may run off, costing you hours of hunting time.

Pre-season conditioning helps a dog maintain its stamina and toughens its feet. Run your dog at least one-half hour several times a week during summer.

TYPES OF HUNTING DOGS

•*Retrievers* include the Labrador retriever, golden retriever, Chesapeake Bay retriever and American water spaniel. These breeds are well-suited for retrieving waterfowl, because their skin secretes an oily substance that sheds water. Most retrievers also flush and retrieve upland game birds.

•*Pointing breeds* include the English Pointer, German short-hair, Brittany spaniel, English setter, Gordon setter and weimaraner. These breeds are used mainly for upland birds, but a few hunters use them for rabbits and squirrels. Many pointers will also retrieve downed game.

•*Flushers* include several types of spaniels, like the springer, cocker and Boykin. These breeds pursue game until it flushes from cover, so they should be trained to work within gun range. The springer is especially popular among pheasant hunters.

•*Hounds,* like the black-and-tan and redtick, have highly sensitive noses and are used mainly for trailing small game. Some, like the beagle, also work well for game birds. Other hounds include the bluetick, Walker and redbone.

Float-Hunting

Water offers hunters an excellent means for approaching game silently. And a float-hunter can cover a large area with relatively little effort.

Float-hunting works best for waterfowl, squirrels, deer, moose and other animals that frequent streambanks and lakeshores. You can also float up on flocks, or *rafts*, of waterfowl in open water.

Most float-hunters use small, low-profile watercraft including jon boats, canoes, semi-Vs and sculling boats. Boats are usually painted camouflage colors or draped with natural vegetation, netting or camouflage cloth.

The best boat depends on the area you hunt and the type of hunting. A jon boat is very stable, but the square bow would not slide through dense cattails. A canoe or double-pointed duck boat is less stable, but would slip through easily. A deep semi-V is best for rough water, but because of its high profile would not be a good choice for floating up on waterfowl. The birds would be less likely to notice a shallow-draft, sculling boat.

Silence is the key to float-hunting success. You can paddle very quietly in a canoe. If you row a boat, make sure the oars do not squeak or scrape the gunwales. Keep loose items tied down and try not to move around in the boat. Wood and fiberglass hulls are quieter than aluminum hulls. Many hunters glue carpet or rubber matting to the bottom, seats and gunwales to muffle sounds.

When you have to travel through cane, cattails, bulrushes or other high vegetation to jump waterfowl and other game, use a push-pole. Some hunters use push-poles as long as 16 feet to propel narrow watercraft through the weeds. If the bottom is soft, use a duck-bill on your push-pole. When you push, the bill spreads, preventing the pole from sinking deep into the mud and causing you to lose leverage. When you pull, the bill closes so it slides easily out of the mud.

Keep safety in mind when float-hunting. Wear a life preserver or sit on a buoyant cushion. Never hunt from a tippy boat. It may flip over if you stand up to shoot or when your dog plunges into the water to retrieve game. To stabilize a canoe or other small watercraft, add *sponsons,* or bands of buoyant material, to the side of the hull. Low-profile boats make you less visible, but they can be dangerous on large, wind-swept waters.

How to Find Downed Game

Losing a wounded animal is one of the greatest frustrations in hunting. Finding downed game requires patience and persistence. But conscientious hunters make every effort to recover game that has been hit.

After the shot, watch the animal closely and try to determine if you made a clean kill, wounded it or missed completely. Clean kills and misses are usually obvious, but it may be more difficult to recognize a wounded animal. Even if you see no sign of a hit, look for hair or feathers, erratic movement or unusual behavior. You might hear the impact when your bullet strikes a big game animal.

Mark the spot where you last saw the animal. Look for an obvious landmark, like a tree, or leave a piece of clothing at the spot. Work outward in widening circles, but return if you fail to find the animal.

Dogs with good retrieving skills greatly improve your chances of finding downed birds and small game. A dog will mark a bird down and promptly retrieve it. If it runs, the dog will circle to pick up the scent, then follow the scent trail.

Follow up any shot at big game, because large animals may show little evidence of being hit. Despite its size, a wounded deer can be as difficult to find as a cottontail. Unless hit in a vital area, it may run a long distance, especially if pursued by hunters.

If you are sure you hit a vital area, begin your pursuit immediately. An animal shot in the heart-lung area will seldom run farther than 100 yards. If you suspect a less damag-

BLOOD TRAILS may provide clues for pursuing wounded game. Bright red, frothy blood indicates a lung shot and tells you to follow immediately. Darker blood usually means a less damaging hit; wait before following.

ing hit, it may be better to wait before following. A bleeding animal may lie down if not pursued. After 30 to 60 minutes, it will probably be too weak to run. Do not wait to follow if rain or snow threatens to obscure the blood trail.

Move quietly and watch ahead for movement when trailing big game. If you fail to see the animal and approach too closely, you may frighten it off, making it more difficult to find. Locating downed game is easiest with two or more hunters. While one inspects the ground for blood, the other looks for any signs of movement. If you lose the trail, mark the spot where you last saw blood. Then you can resume the search at that point.

TIPS FOR FINDING DOWNED BIRDS AND SMALL GAME

•*Check* likely escape routes if you cannot find the animal. Wounded game may slip into a strip of grass connected to the main cover area.

•*Examine* thick clumps of grass or brush patches for signs of the animal. A protruding tail from a patch of cover may be the only evidence of a wounded pheasant.

•*Work* your dog just downwind of downed game. If the dog does not pick up the scent, call it to the spot where you last saw the animal.

HUNTING
WILD GAME

Hunting Big Game

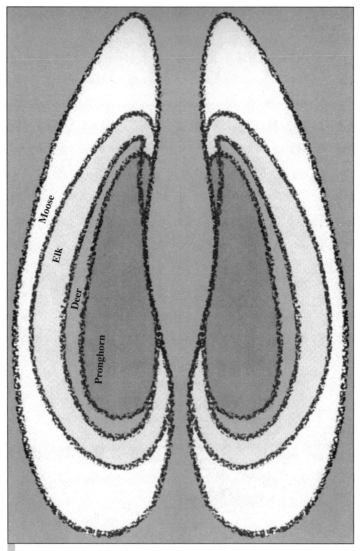

Moose
Elk
Deer
Pronghorn

TRACKS of adult big-game animals vary in size and shape. Moose tracks measure about 5 to 7 inches long; elk tracks 3½ to 5 inches. A moose track is more pointed than that of an elk. Deer tracks range from 2½ to 3½ inches long. Pronghorn tracks approach the size of deer tracks, but have straighter outside edges.

Few sports are as challenging, demanding or rewarding as big-game hunting. Hunters must match wits with animals perfectly adapted to their environment. They often have to walk miles over rugged terrain or carry out carcasses that exceed 1000 pounds. But the rewards are great: a sense of accomplishment, a memorable trophy and a supply of prime-quality meat.

Big-game hunting success depends on an understanding of your quarry. For example, during the rut, many big-game animals lose their normal caution and spend more time away from cover. If you plan your hunt during this brief period, you can greatly improve your chances of bagging a trophy.

Scouting is especially important when hunting big game, because an animal's daily movement is predictable. If you find a fresh trail, a bedding area or feeding site, chances are that game will frequent these spots on subsequent days.

Big-game hunters should know how to use a compass and survival gear. If you hunt in a forest or in the mountains, you could easily become disoriented. Study aerial photos or maps before you hunt a new area and carry them while hunting. By identifying prominent landmarks, you can avoid getting lost. Maps and photos also help you find good hunting spots.

Proper physical conditioning can make hunting more enjoyable, especially if you hunt in steep or mountainous terrain. If you are out of condition or have blisters on your feet, it can be a chore to walk up a hill with a rifle and backpack, let alone drag out a large animal. To get themselves in shape, many hunters jog several times a week during summer. Be sure to break in any new boots before the hunt.

If you shoot a big-game animal, approach it cautiously from behind. Tap the carcass with your foot and be ready to shoot if the animal reacts. Stay away from the rear hooves. Even if the animal appears dead it may kick out of reflex.

Field dress the animal immediately by removing the entrails and windpipe. Begin cooling the carcass as soon as possible. Skinning and hanging the animal will speed the cooling process. You may have to cut up large animals, like moose or elk. Because of its bulk, the whole carcass may retain body heat too long, spoiling the meat. If you must use a

Heart-lung area

SHOOT for the heart-lung area of a big-game animal. The best shot is directly from the side, where the most vital area is exposed. When an animal is quartering toward the hunter, slightly more than half as much vital area is vulnerable; slightly less than half when quartering away. An animal facing the hunter has only a small part of the vital area exposed. Facing away, none of the vital area is vulnerable and the shot would damage too much meat.

bone saw, be extremely careful to keep bits of fat and bone marrow off the meat. They can affect its taste.

Place a rope around the dead animal's neck to drag it out. If the animal is too large to drag, cut it into pieces and carry them out on a packframe. You can also debone the meat to reduce weight.

If the animal has exceptionally large antlers or horns, you may want to have them measured for possible record status with the Boone and Crockett Club or Pope and Young Club. The latter organization maintains records for game killed with bow and arrow. Take precautions so you do not damage the tines or split the skull plate when removing the rack, or when dragging or transporting the carcass.

Every big-game hunter needs to carry more than just a rifle or bow and arrow into the field. Great care must be taken in planning what to carry, however, because if you take too much the load will be uncomfortable to carry; too little, and you may be unprepared for an emergency. Many big-game hunters spending the day in a remote area carry the following items: compass, folding knife, binoculars, canteen, flashlight, space blanket, small mirror for emergency signalling, waterproof matches, tow rope and candy bars. Use the stout cord for tying up a space blanket tarp for temporary shelter.

Whitetail Deer

The whitetail rates as the number one big-game animal in North America. Hunters who pursue all types of big game consider a mature whitetail buck to be the supreme challenge.

Whitetails test a hunter's skill because of their elusive nature. In a Michigan experiment, 39 deer, including 7 bucks, 14 does and 18 fawns, were fenced inside a 1-square-mile area.

Six experienced hunters attempted to find the deer. On the fourth day, one hunter finally spotted a buck. After one month, the average amount of time needed for a hunter to spot a buck was 51 hours. It took an average of 14 hours to spot any deer.

This amazing ability to elude hunters results from the whitetail's keen senses, its ability to hide, and its intimate knowledge of its home range.

Whitetails rely mainly on their sense of smell to detect danger. They can catch a whiff of human scent from blocks away. Deer also hear extremely well. They do not have particularly sharp eyesight, but are quick to detect lateral movement. Deer were once thought to be color blind, but researchers have discovered that deer can perceive some color.

Most hunters find it hard to believe they could walk by a deer only a few feet away. But whitetails regularly elude hunters by sitting tight in grassy or brushy cover. Their coats blend in perfectly.

Deer are so familiar with their surroundings that they can quickly find an escape route or patch of cover. And they are sure to notice any change in their surroundings, like a new deer stand. They will avoid the area for several days until they get used to the new feature.

Whitetails usually attempt to escape danger by sneaking away unnoticed. When alarmed, bucks and does may snort loudly and stamp their feet. This serves as a warning to other deer. If threatened, a deer will bound away with its snowy white tail, or *flag,* erect. But deer normally run only a short distance, then look back to see if they are being pursued. If not, they resume their normal activity.

Deer can attain speeds of 35 to 40 miles per hour and easily jump an 8-foot barrier. If they cannot escape by land, they will take to water. Whitetails are strong swimmers, and have been observed crossing lakes several miles wide.

A whitetail's coat is reddish brown in spring and summer, and brown or gray from fall through winter. Although the underside of the tail is white, the outside is the same color as the rest of the coat and covers up the white rump.

More than two dozen varieties of whitetails inhabit North America. The smallest variety is the Key deer, which generally weighs from 45 to 65 pounds. It lives only in the Florida Keys. The largest variety, the northern whitetail deer, usually weighs from 130 to 190 pounds. It is found in the northeastern states and into southern Canada. The heaviest whitetail on record, 511 pounds, was shot in Minnesota in 1926.

The life-span of a whitetail seldom exceeds 8 years. Most deer taken by hunters are $1\frac{1}{2}$ or $2\frac{1}{2}$ years old. You cannot tell a whitetail's age by its antlers. A $1\frac{1}{2}$-year-old buck may have only spikes, or it may have three or four points per side. Older bucks usually have four or five points on a side.

The record whitetail rack came from a Saskatchewan deer shot in 1993. Both of the main beams measure $28\frac{4}{8}$ inches long. The inside spread was $27\frac{2}{8}$ inches and it scored $213\frac{5}{8}$ Boone and Crockett points.

Whitetails feed primarily on buds and twigs from shrubs and small trees. They also graze on grasses, clover and other green plants. In agricultural areas, they commonly feed on alfalfa, oats, wheat and corn, but will eat almost any crop available.

Does spend the summer and fall with one or two fawns. Mature bucks live alone, except during the breeding season. Whitetails mate between October and January. The rutting period lasts longer in the South than it does in the North. During the rut, bucks become less cautious as they search for does to breed.

Where to Find Whitetails

Whitetails can be found from the conifer forests of Canada to the chaparral plains of Mexico. No other big-game animal can adapt to such a diversity of habitat. The white-tail thrives in farmlands, city suburbs and other areas where human development has severely reduced or eliminated populations of other big game.

Young hardwood forests make prime whitetail habitat because they

DAILY MOVEMENTS during the fall normally begin when deer move into feeding areas like brushy edges, harvested rowcrops, hayfields and fields of green vegetation. They feed until about sunrise, then move to loafing cover like clumps of trees and brush. Or they may retreat to heavier cover like woodlots and wooded creek bottoms. In late afternoon, they return to feeding areas where they stay until after sunset.

provide deer with both food and cover. In a young forest the sunlight can reach the forest floor to grow shrubs and grasses. Whitetails prefer large woodlands, but can survive in smaller areas like woodlots and tree-lined stream corridors.

Farmlands also offer whitetails ample food supplies. They

can support large numbers of deer if they have cover like brushy draws or stream corridors. In both woodlands and farmlands, whitetails often spend the majority of the mid-day hours in the dense cover of neighboring lowland areas such as swamps, bogs and river bottoms.

If you locate a good whitetail area when scouting before the season, chances are the deer will be there when the season begins. Whitetails have a surprisingly small home range. In a Texas study, marked deer were observed over a 5-year period. On the average, does remained within a 1/6-square-mile area. Bucks ranged much more, but stayed within an area averaging 1 2/3 square miles.

Your best chance of seeing whitetails is during feeding periods or when they move between resting and feeding areas. Deer feed most heavily before sunrise and after sunset. They bed down in midday. But season, weather, moon phase and hunting pressure can alter daily movements.

The changing seasons can affect whitetail movements in several ways. As the weather begins to cool in fall, deer feed for longer periods to build up their fat reserves for winter. When the acorns start to fall, deer often feed in the woods rather than move to their usual feeding areas. Movement increases during the rutting period, as bucks wander about in search of does.

Changing weather usually increases deer movement. The animals sense impending weather changes, so they feed heavily while they can. On hot, sunny days, deer spend more time bedded down. They do not necessarily seek cover during a light drizzle. In fact, they often stand out in the open rather than lie in wet grass. But a heavy rain will force them into dense cover, like conifer stands.

During a full moon, whitetails may not come out to feed until after dark. In the dark phase, deer begin feeding earlier. They do not feed as heavily at night, because the lack of light curtails their activity.

Hunting pressure can have a dramatic effect on deer movements. In heavily-hunted areas, whitetails change their feeding schedule once the season begins. They feed earlier and later in the day, or totally at night, to avoid exposing themselves to hunters during shooting hours.

TIPS FOR FINDING WHITETAILS

•*Tracks and droppings* reveal how many deer are using an area. Whitetail pellets are more elongated than those of rabbits and hares.

•*Day trails* wind through thick brush and trees, but seldom cross clearings. Hunters wait along these trails when deer are most active.

•*Night trails* lead through meadows or open croplands. Do not choose a stand along this type of trail, because deer seldom use them in daylight.

•*Rubs* on small saplings result from bucks advertising their presence to other deer by rubbing scent from glands on top of their heads. In an area frequently traveled by a buck a *rub line* often develops.

•*Scrapes* on the ground mean that a buck is attempting to attract does for breeding. As they paw the ground, whitetail bucks often thrash nearby saplings or overhanging branches with their antlers. They check their scrapes regularly, especially those visited by does.

Hunting for Whitetails

Hunters use dozens of techniques to outwit whitetails. Stand-hunting, still-hunting and driving account for the vast majority of deer. But stalking, float-hunting and even unusual methods like antler rattling can be effective.

You can greatly improve your chances by planning your hunt weeks before the season opens. It is possible for an opening-day hunter to leisurely walk into the forest, find a likely-looking spot and bag a trophy buck with-

RATTLING draws bucks during the rut. Take a stand near a dense thicket where you spotted deer the previous day. Or rattle near a fresh scrape, if the spot offers a clear shot. Rub, knock and rattle two antlers together to imitate the sound of fighting bucks. If nothing appears within 15 to 30 minutes, move quietly to another spot.

in minutes. But the odds against such a chance encounter are staggering.

Hunters who enjoy consistent success invest a great deal of time in pre-season scouting. Regardless of how good a spot was in previous years, make sure it still holds good numbers of deer. If you find little sign, look somewhere else. Once you locate a likely area, examine it closely to determine movement paths and escape routes.

Expert deer hunters know not only where, but when to hunt. Wind is an important consideration. You can approach deer more easily if a light breeze rustles the leaves. This background noise makes the sound of your footsteps less noticeable. In a strong wind, deer bed down in cover and stay extra alert.

Some hunters prefer a light rain because it softens the leaves and twigs so they do not crackle underfoot. A light rain provides a low level of background noise, but does not reduce deer activity. In a heavy rain, the animals bed down under dense, overhead cover. Powdery snow makes for quiet walking and good tracking. But when a hard crust develops, deer can hear you coming. Snow-covered tree boughs muffle your sound and may block a deer's vision.

Temperature and cloud cover also affect hunting success, but not the way many hunters think. The common belief is that hunting is best on cool or cloudy days. But after thousands of hours of observation, members of a nation-wide hunting club found that deer move about more when the weather is warm rather than cold, clear rather than cloudy.

Some hunters use bottled scents, either to mask their own odor or to attract deer. Masking scents are made with skunk or fox urine and sprinkled around the stand. Attractants, made from the urine of a doe in heat or various fruits, are spread in the area where you want to shoot your deer.

You do not need high-velocity cartridges for whitetails, because most shots are at close range. Cartridges should be a minimum of .240 caliber with bullets at least 100 grains.

Stand-Hunting for Whitetails

Whitetails are creatures of habit. If you have scouted an area thoroughly and selected a stand near signs of recent deer activity, you can be sure that whitetails will eventually pass your way. If you lose confidence, become impatient and decide to go after the deer, you significantly reduce your odds.

Choose a stand that offers good visibility. It should be located where the wind will not blow your scent toward a trail or other spot where you expect to see deer. You should also select a spot where the sun will not shine in your eyes. Be sure you are concealed on the sides from which deer will most likely approach.

But deer may not come from the direction you expect, so you must slowly scan in a complete circle around your stand. When you spot a deer at a distance, stay motionless and be patient. If you see a doe, watch closely because there may be a buck trailing behind.

If you hunt in the morning, walk to your stand very quietly. Be sure to get there while it is still dark. Most hunters stay at their stand until about two hours after sunrise. But it often pays to wait a little longer. The commotion caused by other hunters leaving their stands may spook deer to you. If you hunt in the afternoon, stay until the close of shooting hours. Hunters often see more deer in the final minutes than during the rest of the day.

TIPS FOR STAND-HUNTING

•*Elevated stands* place you above a deer's usual vision level. They also expand your field of view and keep your scent above the ground. But many hunters simply hide behind a tree, or a pile of logs or brush.

•*Tower blinds* make it possible to hunt from a high elevation where there are no tall trees. Some tower blinds are permanent.

•*Intersections* of two or more heavily-used trails make prime stand-hunting locations. Another good spot is an area with many fresh scrapes or rubs.

•*Raise* and lower your unloaded gun or bow with a rope when hunting from an elevated stand. Make sure the barrel is pointed away from you.

Still-Hunting for Whitetails

Of all the whitetail hunting techniques, still-hunting is the most difficult to master. But the challenge of trying to find a weak spot in the deer's ironclad defense system appeals to many hunters.

Still-hunting works best when whitetails are moving between bedding and feeding sites. Most hunters prefer damp weather and a light wind to obscure the sound of their footsteps.

The slower you move, the more deer you will see. Look for signs like the flick of an ear, the glint off an antler, or the white throat patch of a deer. A bedded whitetail will often sit tight while a hunter passes within a few yards. Place each step carefully; plant your toe first, then gradually lower your heel. Try to avoid twigs and leaves. Stop after a few steps, then slowly move your head to examine the terrain. Bend down from time to time to scan the ground below the leaf line.

If you accidentally make a noise, stop moving immediately. If they do not detect motion, whitetails will usually forget the disturbance within a few minutes. Many hunters prefer to still-hunt on trails because they can move more quietly. Most trails are packed down, so you do not crunch leaves. They also have less brush to scrape against your clothes.

Always walk against the wind so your scent does not precede you through the woods. This method will also help you sneak up on feeding deer. They usually face into the wind and will not see you coming.

To still-hunt in a field of standing corn, walk across the

DEER DRIVES are an effective way to hunt whitetails throughout much of North America. Typically, a deer runs for a short period of time when jumped by drivers, then slows to a walk. Ideally, posters are in place to intercept the deer as it walks by.

rows, peeking both ways down each row. Whitetails often feed and bed in standing rowcrops. The technique works best on breezy days; the rustling stalks prevent deer from hearing you.

Driving for Whitetails

The success of a deer drive depends on good organization. A group of hunters wandering haphazardly through the woods has little hope of shooting deer.

Every drive should have a leader who is familiar with the

terrain. Before the drive, the leader gives clear instructions to each hunter. Posters take their stands first; each should wait in a spot with a good view, preferably from an elevated stand. Drivers synchronize their watches, then spread out across the upwind side of cover. Distance between the drivers may be only 15 yards in dense cover or more than 50 yards if the cover is sparse.

At the appointed time, drivers begin walking downwind. Deer soon detect the hunter's scent. They will flush closer if drivers move quietly. Some deer move ahead, some double back, and others remain bedded down.

Driving will work anytime deer are in cover. But if you drive a block of cover too large, whitetails will slip to the side and let the drivers pass.

Deer drives can be dangerous. Limit the number of hunters so you can keep track of everyone's location. Posters in elevated stands also make a drive safer. Their shots angle toward the ground, and they are above the normal shooting plane of the drivers.

TIPS FOR DRIVING DEER

•*Choose* a drive leader before any drive begins. The hunter with the most experience in the area is usually the best choice.

•*Keep* adjacent drivers in sight at all times. This prevents a hunter from moving too far ahead of the others and into the firing zone. Blaze orange clothing is mandatory.

•*Post* near a known escape route. Deer often move from one block of woods to another by sneaking through a connecting patch of lighter cover.

•*Watch* closely for whitetails doubling back through the driving line. Deer may sneak back though drivers are visible on both sides. As drivers approach posters, deer must double back or break into the open.

Mule Deer

MULE DEER antlers are generally taller and have a greater spread than those of whitetail deer. On a good-sized mule deer, each fork will branch again for a minimum of four points per side.

The mule deer's popularity is unrivaled among western big game. The animal is named for its mulelike ears, which may measure a foot long. Muleys look much like whitetails, but differ greatly in behavior and personality.

You can tell a mule deer from a whitetail by the black tip on its tail. Most of the muley's tail is white, making the rump patch more evident than it is on whitetails. The antlers also differ. The main beam of a mule deer antler is forked; whitetails have a continuous main beam.

The record mule deer rack has a spread of 30⅞ inches. Its right antler has six points and a main beam that measures 30⅛ inches long; its left has five points and totals 28¾ inches. The animal was shot in Colorado in 1972.

Like whitetails, mule deer have excellent senses of smell and hearing. But muleys have better long-distance vision. They usually bed down where they have a good view of the surrounding terrain. Unlike whitetails, they rarely sit tight and let hunters pass only yards away.

When they detect something unusual, mule deer cock their large ears to pinpoint the direction of the disturbance. Then they bound off in pogo-stick fashion, with all four feet touching the ground simultaneously. This distinctive gait, called *stotting*, enables them to survey the terrain better and to change direction instantly.

A startled mule deer will run much farther than a whitetail, sometimes up to 4 miles. They usually bound uphill, sometimes pausing for a last look before slipping over a ridge. Muleys normally run with their tails down.

Compared to whitetails, mule deer have a calm disposition. They show little fear of man as long as enough distance separates them. But they become nervous and often slip away when a hunter disappears from sight.

Mule deer prefer terrain more open than that used by whitetails. Mountains and foothills with sparse stands of timber, rolling prairies broken by canyons and coulees, and low brushlands make ideal habitat.

Where mule deer and whitetails coexist, they eat many of the same foods. But the mule deer's diet usually differs because of the rougher terrain. Common foods include bitterbrush, mountain mahogany, serviceberry, chokecherry and sagebrush.

Early morning and late afternoon are the prime feeding periods of mule deer. Favorite areas are brushy hillsides, meadows, croplands and pastures, generally at lower elevations than bedding areas.

Mule deer move as much as 2 miles from feeding to bedding areas. In midday, they often bed down on the lee side of a break. They may rest just below the crest of a hill or the lip of a ravine. They watch only the downhill side, relying on the wind to bring them the scent of anything approaching from behind. Mule deer will also bed on a grassy mountain terrace, in the bottom of a dry wash, or near a tree on a hillside. In remote areas, they may feed in the open rather than bed down during the day.

After a rainy period, look for mule deer on sunny hillsides. Heavy snow drives them from the mountains to lower ground. Herds migrate as far as 50 miles, often wintering in brushy draws and canyons blown free of snow.

Mule deer often form large herds. Small and medium-sized bucks mix with does and fawns, but the largest bucks are usually loners.

Most mule deer breed in November and December, but the breeding period may be as early as October or as late as March. During the rut, the bucks thrash or horn bushes,

HEAVY SNOW often pushes mule deer from high elevations to lower ground.

poles, branches and tree trunks in a display of dominance. They do not make scrapes.

Seven varieties of mule deer inhabit the western third of North America. The desert mule deer ranges as far south as central Mexico. The most numerous variety, the Rocky Mountain mule deer, is found as far north as the Northwest Territories.

Rocky Mountain mule deer reach the largest size, generally weighing from 140 to 200 pounds. The largest on record, 453 pounds, was taken in Montana. The southern mule deer is the smallest variety; it weighs from 85 to 110 pounds.

Blacktail deer, although closely related to mule deer, are darker, generally smaller and have ears only 6 to 7 inches long. They live in steep, heavily-forested terrain along the Pacific Coast. They behave more like whitetails.

Hunting for Mule Deer

Most hunters find it easier to outsmart a mule deer than a whitetail. The muley's less secretive nature and penchant for open terrain often tip the scales in favor of the hunter. But a big buck mule deer can be just as elusive as a trophy whitetail.

When hunting in hilly or mountainous terrain, get to the highest part of your hunting area early in the morning, preferably before shooting hours. Your chances of spotting muleys in the open are best in the morning, and the high elevation gives you a good view.

Glass every detail of the landscape. Mule deer blend in well with their surroundings and are masters at concealing themselves in a small amount of cover. If you spot one animal, look closely for others because mule deer often feed and bed in groups.

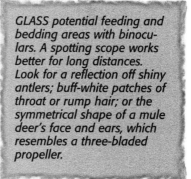

GLASS potential feeding and bedding areas with binoculars. A spotting scope works better for long distances. Look for a reflection off shiny antlers; buff-white patches of throat or rump hair; or the symmetrical shape of a mule deer's face and ears, which resembles a three-bladed propeller.

If the animal is too far away for a shot, plan a stalk. Use natural features of the landscape, like ravines, for conceal-ment. Try to approach from above, because muleys expect danger from below.

Should glassing prove futile, begin still-hunting your way downhill. Some hunters take stands along trails where muleys are likely to pass. When hunting with companions, driving can be effective.

A running mule deer makes a difficult target because of its bounding gait and unpredictable turns. But it may stop and look back if you shout or whistle. Be ready for a standing shot as it nears the top of a ridge or a stand of timber. A muley sometimes stops just before it disappears.

Mule deer hunters take shots up to 300 yards, so sight in your rifle for long-range shooting. Use a high-velocity cartridge of at least .240 caliber with a minimum bullet weight of 80 grains.

TIPS FOR HUNTING MULE DEER

•*Stand-hunt* along corridors between feeding and bedding areas. Conceal yourself behind a natural feature like a rock outcrop or large tree, or use a tree stand. Mule deer trails are usually less distinct than those of whitetails. But the animals often follow natural passes like a saddle between two ridges.

•*Still-hunt* a series of ravines by starting at the head of one ravine, then walking the edge. Look over the crest periodi-cally to spot bedded deer. Cross the ravine at the lower end and walk the other side to check for deer you may have missed. Then, cross to the head of the next ravine and repeat the procedure.

•*Drive* for mule deer in ravines. One hunter walks up the bottom and another halfway up the side. A third hunter posts at the head of the ravine. Driving also works well along wooded or brushy stream corridors.

•*Never* shoot at a deer when it is on top of a ridge. Always be sure there is a solid backstop behind the animal before shooting. Remember an animal is not a safe backstop. Bullets will travel completely through it.

Elk

Prized for its magnificent antlers and delectable meat, a bull elk is the big game hunter's greatest trophy. A large animal may have antlers five feet long.

Antlers of the largest bulls, called *monarchs*, have eight points on a side. *Imperial* elk have seven points per side, and *royal* elk six. The record elk rack has eight points on one side and seven on the other. The main beam of one antler measures 59⅝ inches; the other 55⅝ inches. The rack, which has a 45½-inch spread, came from an elk taken in Colorado in 1899.

Two varieties of elk provide the vast majority of hunting. Most numerous is the Rocky Mountain elk. The slightly larger Roosevelt elk lives in the coastal mountains of the

BUGLING takes place during the rut. It consists of a series of melodious whistles, progressing from low to high pitch. Herd bulls bugle to intimidate competing males. Challengers bugle to lure the herd bull away from his harem. In addition to bugling, herd bulls bellow, rake trees with their antlers, and spar with other bulls to drive them off. Occasionally, two bulls ram each other and lock antlers in a test of strength.

Pacific Northwest. Elk are brownish-gray with long, chestnut-brown hair on the neck. The tail and rump patch are buff-white. Bulls average about 750 pounds and stand 5 feet high at the shoulder. Cows weigh about one-fourth less.

Elk prefer heavily-timbered country broken by clearcuts, burns, and meadows, called *parks*. The best habitat is in remote, mountainous terrain laced with streams and small glacial lakes. Elk have large territories and will not tolerate human disturbance.

Cow elk live in large herds which also include calves and an occasional spike bull. An old cow leads the herd, alerting the others to danger with a sharp bark. Older bulls live alone or in small groups of up to six. Bulls wander more than cows, shunning cow herds until the mating season.

The rut usually begins in early September. A dominant bull, called a *herd bull*, assembles a harem of up to 30 cows. He protects them from the advances of younger males, or of other herd bulls.

To detect danger, elk rely mainly on a keen sense of smell. They also have excellent hearing. On windy days, when swishing tree limbs would obscure the sound of a hunter's approach, they become nervous and retreat to heavy cover. Elk quickly notice movement, but usually ignore stationary objects.

An elk can run 35 miles-per-hour in a short burst and can maintain a 15 to 20 miles-per-hour trot over a long distance. A running bull carries his nose high, so his antlers lay back along his body and do not tangle in branches. Elk are strong swimmers and can jump obstructions up to 10 feet high.

Elk feed mainly on grasses. As winter nears, they consume more twigs and leaves from shrubs and trees. The morning feeding period begins about 1 hour before sunrise and lasts until 1 hour after. In late afternoon, they begin feeding about 2 hours before sunset and continue until dark. Elk usually have four or five shorter feeding periods during the day, each lasting from 15 minutes to 1 hour. Because they eat so often, elk usually bed within a mile of where they feed. They prefer bedding areas with a good view, like a grassy terrace on a hillside.

> MIGRATIONS in late fall begin when snow depth reaches 18 inches or more, and temperatures plunge below zero. Elk move to snow-free, south-facing slopes at lower elevations.

In summer and early fall, elk scatter over a large area at high elevation. The rugged terrain prevents intrusion by humans. In late fall, heavy snow and extreme cold push elk to lower levations. But with a break in the weather, they may return to high altitudes. Some herds move 100 miles to find the right conditions.

SIGNS OF ELK ACTIVITY

•*Droppings* that are elongated and 3/4 to 1½ inches in length mean that elk have been browsing on twigs and leaves. Droppings in a large mass are from elk that have eaten green grass.

•*Wallows* are made by big bulls to announce their presence to cows. A bull scrapes out a depression at a spring seep. He urinates in the mud, then rolls in it, plastering his body.

•*Fresh rubs* during the rut also advertise a large bull's presence. Elk rubs are higher than those made by deer, and the bark of the sapling is stripped over a greater length.

Hunting for Elk

A successful elk hunter must earn his trophy. Unlike most other big game animals, elk will retreat deep into the forest or climb to extreme elevations to escape hunting pressure. Seldom can you drive to your hunting area and hope to bag an elk.

Elk hunters often spend several days in the mountains. They scout a prospective area to find fresh elk sign, then set up camp at least one-half mile away.

Scent helps hunters locate areas used by elk. The animals emit a strong, musky odor, similar to the smell of sheep. The scent lingers in bedding or wallowing areas long after the elk leave.

PACK TRAINS enable hunters to reach the remote, mountainous areas which offer the best elk hunting. Horses or mules also simplify the task of carrying out the antlers and cut-up carcasses.

Daily movement patterns of elk depend on hunting pressure. When not disturbed, elk feed in open meadows or areas with young trees and shrubs. They bed down at the edge of timber nearby. If threatened, they move up to 5 miles into the timber after feeding. Or they may retreat to a steep, conifer-studded slope where they sniff rising air currents to detect danger from below.

One of the most productive techniques is stand-hunting in early morning and late afternoon. For a morning hunt, walk to your stand in the dark, moving quietly to avoid spooking any elk in the vicinity. Remain on your stand until about 2 hours after sunrise, glassing to find elk that you could stalk. In the afternoon, be on your stand at least 2 hours before sunset.

In midday, when elk are bedded down, you are more likely to see them by still-hunting. The technique works best when the ground is damp or covered with soft snow. In dry woods, it is nearly impossible to walk quietly enough to approach within gun range.

Driving can also be effective, but only if your hunting party is familiar with the terrain. Drivers approach from below a known bedding area and push the elk uphill to posters. The posters station themselves along game trails in thick timber or near clearings where elk are likely to break into the open. A startled elk will make plenty of noise. But more often, they slip away silently, so posters must watch closely.

During the rut, hunters can bugle in bull elk. Many elk calls mimic the high-pitched, squeaky whistle of a spike bull. This call infuriates the herd bull. He thinks an unworthy youngster is making a play for his harem, so he moves toward the caller, ready to do battle. If a bull answers but does not move, he is probably guarding his harem and reluctant to leave. In this case, try stalking close enough for a shot. Perhaps the easiest way to learn how to call elk is to purchase one of the many instructional tapes offered by the major hunting call manufacturers.

Because elk are so large and shooting distances so long, most hunters prefer high-velocity cartridges of .270 caliber or larger. Use a bullet weighing at least 150 grains.

ELK HUNTING TECHNIQUES

•*Bugle* for elk starting at dawn. When a bull answers, move toward him, staying downwind and calling about every 5 minutes as long as he continues to respond. Keep approaching until you get within about 400 yards. Then select a blind and continue calling to lure him within shooting range.

•*Stand-hunt* above trails or wallows, or at the edge of a meadow where elk feed. Trails and feeding areas are most productive in early morning and late afternoon. Bulls usually visit wallows late in the day.

•*Still-hunt* to within shooting range. Bowhunters often get as close as 20 yards. Start by walking a ridge, looking for elk on terraces or hillsides. Approach elk from above because they usually watch the downhill side.

•*Follow* fresh elk tracks in the snow. Stay on the trail as long as it goes downhill; stay above the trail if it moves across the slope. Constantly look ahead so you see the animal before it sees you.

Moose

With antlers towering 10 feet above the ground, a bull moose is truly an awesome sight. A large bull weighs 1200 pounds, and moose up to 1800 pounds have been recorded. The world-record rack has a 65⅛-inch spread. The right *palm* measures 54⁴/₈ inches and has 19 points; the left 53⁶/₈ inches with 15 points.

Like other members of the deer family, moose have an excellent sense of smell and good hearing. But their eyesight is poorer than that of deer. Moose seldom notice a nearby hunter if he does not move.

Despite their size, moose can run up to 30 miles per hour. When spooked, they will crash through brush and small trees, ignoring trails. But moose can also slip quietly through cover to elude a hunter.

Young hardwood forests with scattered conifers, and brushy lowlands make ideal moose habitat. The dense undergrowth provides ample food and bedding cover. But they can also live in older forests with little underbrush.

A big bull can browse on vegetation up to 11 feet off the ground. If it cannot reach the upper portion of a small tree, a moose will straddle the trunk, then start walking. The animal bends down the tree, feeding on leaves and twigs as it walks.

Moose feed most heavily from just before sunrise to about 2 hours after and again in late afternoon. But they may feed anytime during the day or night. When not feeding, moose bed down in the thickets.

MOOSE have a dark brown, almost black, coat. A large bull stands 7 feet tall at the shoulder and measures 10 feet in length. Each antler has a large palm with numerous points along the outer edge. Moose usually stay near water. Bogs and lakes provide a source of food, a place to cool off and a refuge from swarms of insects. Excellent swimmers, moose will not hesitate to cross a fast river or even a large lake.

Most of the year, moose live by themselves. They lead docile lives, seldom moving more than one-half mile in a day, but during the rut, which begins in September, bulls become ill-tempered. They have been known to attack cars and even trains. Rutting bulls regularly visit wallows. Both sexes roam widely during the rut, sometimes wandering over 10 miles from their usual home range.

Hunters see the most moose on clear, calm days. Heavy overcast, rain, snow or high winds keep the animals bedded down.

Before you hunt, scout the area for sign. With animals of this size, the evidence will be obvious. Select a stand near a wallow, a well-used stream crossing, or any spot where the topography funnels moose through a small area. Get to your stand before daylight, remain until mid-morning, then return in late afternoon.

Still-hunting can be effective in midday, especially if there is snow to quiet your footsteps. If you attempt to sneak through heavy timber and brush, you will make too much noise. During the rut, antler rattling or calling may lure bulls from dense cover. Using cupped hands or a birch-bark megaphone, make a series of short grunts to imitate a cow in heat. If you hear a response, pour water in a puddle to imitate a cow urinating.

In hilly or mountainous country, hunters stalk moose after spotting them with binoculars. Glass for moose along forest edges, in willow swamps or near other feeding areas. Get to your vantage point early, so you can complete your stalk before the animals retreat to bedding areas.

Float-hunting works well along streams and lakeshores. The technique works best in early morning and late after-noon, when moose come to drink and to feed on shore-line willows.

Most moose hunters use large-caliber rifles and high-velocity ammunition, similar to those used for elk. A moose may not drop immediately after the shot. To prevent losing a wounded animal, wait 10 to 15 minutes for it to lie down, then begin pursuing it.

TIPS FOR FINDING MOOSE

•*Broken saplings* indicate a bull moose in rut. A bull twists off saplings with his antlers to advertise his presence to cows.

•*Droppings* measure 1 to 1½ inches long. When moose are eating browse, droppings have a consistency similar to compressed sawdust.

•*Brushy lowlands* are favorite feeding areas. Moose prefer red-osier dogwood, willow, aspen, birch, mountain ash and aquatic plants.

Pronghorns

The pronghorn's astonishing speed and superb vision are unmatched among North American big-game animals. Hunters refer to pronghorns as antelope but they are not related to the antelope of Africa. They have no living relatives in the animal kingdom.

Pronghorns get their name from the sharp prongs that project forward on the horns of bucks. Their upper body is tan; the underside and rump white. Most antelope weigh 80 to 130 pounds, with the largest bucks weighing up to 140. The record pronghorn rack has a right horn measuring 17⁶/8 inches in length. Its left horn totals 17⁴/8 inches long. The animal was shot in Arizona in 1985.

The fleet-footed pronghorn can reach a speed of 60 miles per hour. Special adaptations for stamina such as an oversized windpipe and large lung capacity compared to their body size enable pronghorns to maintain high speeds for several miles. Their large, protruding eyeballs are approximately 2 inches in diameter, and their vision compares to that of a man looking through 8x binoculars.

Pronghorns prefer open plains, prairies and treeless foothills. The best habitat has rolling hills sprinkled with water holes and ample sagebrush for food. Pronghorns also eat forbs, brush and occasionally grasses. They feed most heavily in early morning and late afternoon, but may graze anytime day or night. During the spring and early summer pronghorns get most of their water needs met from succulent vegetation in their diet, but in the dry seasons of mid-summer and fall they will go to a water hole at least once a day.

Their wary, nervous temperament is consistent with other prey animals, and they are constantly on the look-out for any signs of danger. The pronghorn's sense of smell is good; however, sight and speed are their primary defenses. When alarmed, an antelope flares its white rump hairs or makes a barking sound, alerting others in the herd. Contrary, however, to their skittish nature, pronghorns are remarkably curious and may move a considerable distance to investigate an unusual sight.

Rutting begins in August in northern pronghorn range and may occur as late as November in the south. In spring, mature dominant bucks claim territories that contain the best food and water. They vigorously defend the territory against other intruding bucks. As the rut approaches, the dominant or herd buck attempts to gather and keep a large harem of does in his territory, breeding each when she comes into estrus. Pronghorn buck fights, as the herd buck chases intruding bucks away, seldom result in serious injury. These distractions may last long enough for a hunter to stalk within range.

Spot-and-stalk is the primary tactic when hunting prong-horns. The hunter glasses, with binoculars or a spotting scope, from a high point of ground. After a good buck is spotted, a stalk, utilizing any available cover, is planned to get within shooting range.

Stand-hunting tactics can be used if a herd shows repeated daily movement patterns. Some hunters set up a blind and wait near a well-used waterhole or fence crossing. Although they are perfectly capable of jumping fences, pronghorns prefer to go under or through them. They habitually cross at the same places, leaving hair on the barbed wire or on the ground. Stand-hunting near these locations is often productive.

A gun hunter using a flat-shooting scoped rifle need only get within about 300 yards or so of a pronghorn. Bowhunters

IDENTIFY bucks by their black cheek patch. Mature bucks have horns that extend above the ears. Some does have buttons or spikes, but they are shorter than the ears.

must get much closer and have developed methods to overcome the limited range of their weapons. Decoying can be an effective method when the bucks are rutting. The hunter puts up the buck decoy within sight of a dominant buck, hiding behind it, hoping that the antelope will challenge this intruder. Antelope calls may also be used, when decoying, to challenge aggresive bucks. Calls may be used by a gun hunter. Decoys should never be used by any hunter during an open gun season.

TIPS FOR HUNTING PRONGHORN

•*Locate* pronghorns by glassing from a ridge. Sneak quietly to the edge, because there may be antelope on the other side. Use a spotting scope to check horn length.

•*Stalk* to within shooting range by creeping just below a rise. Grass or brush will break up your outline.

•*Stand-hunt* from a blind near a water hole or fence crossing. Or simply hide in a depression.

•*Challenge* a rutting buck during the archery season using a buck decoy. Never use a decoy during gun season.

Black Bear

Of all big-game animals, bear are the most misunderstood. Some people regard them as fun-loving clowns. Others envision them as blood-thirsty killers. Records exist of black bear attacking humans, but they usually make every effort to avoid man.

Black bear favor mixed conifer and hardwood forests, with clearings that produce food. A bear's diet consists mainly of berries, fruits, nuts, grasses, corn and other crops. But they also eat insects, small mammals and fish. In spring, they may feed on carcasses of animals killed by severe winter weather. They frequently gorge themselves at garbage dumps. Bear have an enormous appetite in late summer and fall. They often gain over 100 pounds in preparation for hibernation.

Bear feed most heavily during cool morning and evening hours. They remain in shady areas on hot days because their dark fur absorbs too much heat from the sun. Windy or rainy weather also reduces their activity.

With the exception of the June breeding season, males, or *boars*, lead solitary lives. *Sows* stay with cubs for about 1 1/2 years. While most black bear have territories from 5 to 15 square miles, some boars have been known to range up to 100 square miles.

In the North, bear begin hibernating as early as September. They remain in their dens until April, although they occasionally wander about during a warm spell. In warmer climates, bear may not hibernate. If they do, hibernation begins later and does not last as long.

Black bear have many color phases. Most are glossy black, brown, or cinnamon, but they may be white or even bluish.

A large boar weighs 300 to 400 pounds; some exceed 600. Sows weigh about one third less. The largest black bear on record weighed 802 pounds. It was taken in Wisconsin in 1885.

Biologists rate the bear among the most intelligent game animals. A bear can run 25 miles per hour and climb a tree in seconds. They rely mainly on a keen sense of smell to find food and detect danger. They have excellent hearing, but poor eyesight.

Even in good bear country, the animals are not abundant, averaging only one bear for every 2 square miles. Because bear are so scattered, hunters employ techniques seldom used for other big game.

Baiting takes advantage of the bear's highly developed sense of smell. A bear can detect the scent of bait from over one-half mile away and will come to the hunter's stand. This method works in spring when hungry bear emerge from dens, and in fall when they feed heavily to build up fat reserves.

Some bear hunters use hounds, such as Walkers, black-and-tans, or Plotts. But many people consider the use of dogs unsporting, and in some states it is illegal. Those who object maintain that the bear has no chance. In reality, however, it often wins. A bear can run for miles and often loses the dogs. When cornered, it can quickly dispatch a hound. Some hunters pursue bear solely for the sport of the chase. Once an animal is treed or brought to bay, they call off the dogs and let it go.

Still-hunting in feeding areas accounts for some bear, but the odds of randomly walking up on an animal are slim. They are too wary and their populations too sparse.

Bear hunters use rifles of at least .30 caliber. You can kill a bear with a smaller caliber, but a larger caliber reduces the chances of a bear attacking after the shot. Bullets should weigh at least 165 grains.

SIGNS OF BEAR ACTIVITY

•*Damaged trees or bushes* are common feeding signs. A bear rips down a branch with its claws, then strips off the fruit or berries.

•*Tracks* have distinct claw marks and measure 3½ to 5 inches wide. The front foot is 4 to 5 inches long; the hind foot 6 to 7 inches.

•*Droppings* reveal what bear have been eating. They often contain berries, grass, hair and wood eaten along with insects.

BEAR HUNTING TECHNIQUES

•*Bait* black bear with food scraps. Cover each bait station with logs to keep out smaller scavengers. Bait several different locations before the season, then select a stand near a bait-site that bear visit regularly.

•*Follow* hounds on foot or horseback until they tree or corner a bear. Hunters scout a potential area to locate fresh tracks, then release the dogs. Even if the scent is cold, good dogs will pick up the bear's trail.

Hunting Small Game

The nation's hunters spend more time in pursuit of small game than on any other type of hunting. The sport's popularity stems from the relative ease of finding game. With a little scouting, you can probably locate small game within a few miles of your home. Even with a minimum of equipment, you can bring home a tasty meal.

In this book, the term *small game* includes only the small mammals commonly hunted for sport and food, namely rabbit, hare, squirrel and raccoon.

Even the novice has a reasonable chance to bag rabbits or squirrels. But this does not mean that small game hunting is easy. Your success will improve as your level of skill increases. And you can apply the skills you gain to other types of hunting.

Small-game hunters have ample opportunity to enjoy their sport. Most hunting seasons last at least 6 months, and some are continuous. Because you can find these animals close to home, you can make frequent short trips, which is difficult when hunting most other types of game. Almost all states and provinces have liberal bag limits.

Most hunters use shotguns or .22 caliber rimfire rifles. But some prefer a combination gun with a .22 caliber rifle barrel on top and a 20 gauge shotgun barrel on the bottom. Combination guns are ideal for small game because you can fire one barrel at standing animals and the other at

running targets. Hunters also use small-caliber centerfire rifles, muzzleloading rifles and shotguns, and bows with blunt-tipped arrows.

A pair of waterproof leather boots is a good investment. With the possible exceptions of brush pants, a burr-proof jacket with a game pouch, binoculars, and a small knife for field dressing, you need little other equipment.

Many hunters compare rabbit and squirrel meat to chicken. Raccoon tends to be oily and has a distinctive flavor of its own. Small game tastes better if you remove the entrails soon after killing the animal.

Cottontail Rabbits

Each year, hunters throughout the United States bag 30 to 40 million cottontail rabbits. This staggering total results from the cottontail's tremendous reproductive rate, and its ability to adapt to a wide range of habitats and foods.

COTTONTAILS are named for their fluffy white tail. The fur on the upper part of the body is grayish-brown with black tips. The undersides are white. Adults measure 14 to 19 inches long and weigh 2½ to 3½ pounds.

Cottontails breed in the spring and summer, producing up to eight litters, each with three to six young. They prefer brushy edges and woodlots, but can live almost anywhere with the exception of dense forests. They eat practically any type of green plant. When green vegetation dies back, they switch to twigs and bark.

Rabbits start feeding before dawn and continue for 2 or 3 hours. They resume feeding at sunset. They move about most on calm, sunny days. Rain or wind drives them into heavy cover.

A cottontail spends most of the day sitting in a *form*, a shallow depression in grass or snow. The grass eventually wears away, or the snow melts down and compacts. Often a form is concealed by overhanging grass or other type of overhead cover.

Rabbits use their superb hearing to sense impending danger. To escape, they bolt away on established travel lanes. Cottontails run in an elusive, zig-zag pattern, but their speed is not as fast as many hunters believe. They normally run 12 to 15 miles per hour, but can reach 20.

Normally, cottontails will not run far. They spend their entire lives within a few acres, getting to know every feature of that area. Rather than run straight away, a rabbit will circle so it can stay in familiar territory. When frightened, it will often slip into a woodchuck burrow or brush pile.

You can bag some cottontails by walking through likely cover, looking for rabbits in their forms. Upland bird hunters frequently flush rabbits by moving in typical walk-and-wait fashion. Like most game animals, a cottontail becomes nervous when a nearby hunter stands motionless, and it will often bound from its resting spot.

Strip cover, like brushy fencelines and hedgerows, makes ideal cottontail habitat. The brush and high grass provide food and cover. Abandoned farms also offer a variety of hiding spots. Look for rabbits around groves, under old machinery or in tall grass. Brush piles provide good escape cover. A fox or owl would have little chance of reaching a rabbit beneath the logs and sticks.

Hunting with dogs offers an interesting and effective alternative. Release the dogs where you find plenty of sign. Beagles have excellent noses and will scour the ground thoroughly to find fresh scent. They will methodically follow the trail, slowly pushing the rabbit ahead.

Wait in the area where the dogs first detect fresh scent. A rabbit will usually circle and return to the spot where it was flushed. If it does not circle, try to predict its escape route, then attempt to intercept it. Almost any dog will chase cottontails, but if it works too fast, the rabbit will dash under a brush pile or down a hole.

Rabbits may contract a bacterial disease called tularemia, which causes them to behave listlessly and eventually kills them. But the disease is rare. One researcher found it in only 2 of 12,000 rabbits he examined. Nevertheless, refrain from shooting rabbits that move slowly or otherwise behave unusually. Tularemia can be transmitted to humans who eat or handle the flesh of infected animals.

To hit zig-zagging cottontails, most hunters use shotguns with modified or improved cylinder chokes, and No. 6 shot. But when rabbits are in their forms or feeding in the open, a .22 rifle with a scope may enable you to get a shot before they spook.

SIGNS OF COTTONTAIL ACTIVITY

•*Tracks* of cottontails have side-by-side hind prints ahead of smaller front prints. One front foot falls ahead of the other.

•*Runways* in tall grass serve as escape routes. Rabbits usually follow the same paths through cover, eventually matting down the vegetation.

•*Feeding signs* include girdled shrubs or saplings, and cleanly-snipped twigs. Cottontails prefer the bark of sumac and fruit trees.

COTTONTAIL HUNTING TIPS

•*Locate* a form with fresh sign. Droppings are round and about 3/8-inch across. A rabbit will seldom move far from its form.

•*Walk* around the form in ever-widening circles. Look for

the rabbit in clumps of brush, around the bases of trees, in tall grass or in any dense cover. Continue walking until you cover the entire area within a 100-foot radius of the cottontail's form. Follow any fresh tracks you encounter.

•*Watch* for rabbit tracks as you walk a strip of cover like a brushy fenceline. A retriever or flushing dog will scare up tight-holding rabbits.

•*Hunt* around abandoned farmsteads. Look for rabbits as you round the corner of a building and be ready for a quick shot.

•*Flush* cottontails by beating a brush pile with a stick. Or climb on top of the brush pile, jump up and down, and yell to scare out rabbits.

Snowshoe Hares

The snowshoe is named for its oversized hind feet, which provide a large surface area to support the animal on soft snow.

Noted for their dramatic cycles of abundance, snowshoe populations have been known to peak at 3400 animals per square mile. Following a peak year, the population often declines to such a low level that hunters have difficulty finding enough animals to hunt. A complete cycle takes about 10 years.

Snowshoes behave much like cotton-tails and eat similar foods. But they are more likely to feed at night. They prefer conifer swamps and young hardwood forests rather than brushy edges. Snowshoes are larger, faster and better jumpers.

Hunting with hounds works as well for showshoes as it does for cotton-tails. Most hunters use beagles, but a breed with longer legs will have less trouble pushing through deep snow. Like cottontails, snowshoes will stay ahead of a dog and circle back toward a waiting hunter.

Snowshoe hunters generally use shotguns with improved cylinder or modified chokes, and No. 4 to 6 shot. A snow-shoe can run up to 30 miles per hour and change direction quickly, so a tight choke is less effective. To increase their shooting range, many still-hunters use .22 rifles.

SNOWSHOES, also called varying hares, *vary in color depending on the season. The coat is white in winter and brown in summer (inset). Snowshoes are 16 to 21 inches long and weigh 3 to 4 pounds.*

HUNTING TIPS

•*Look* for a snowshoe's black eye and black-tipped ears when hunting in snow. You can spot the animals more easily after a mid-winter thaw, because their white bodies stand out against bare ground.

•*Follow* tracks after a fresh snowfall. About 2 inches of new snow over a hard crust makes for ideal tracking. If the snow is more than a foot deep, a pair of snowshoes will make walking much easier.

Gray Squirrels

A gray squirrel leaping through the treetops will test the marksmanship of any hunter. Using their wide-angle vision and sharp hearing, squirrels quickly detect a hunter, then scurry away before he can shoot.

To avoid being seen, a squirrel moves to the opposite side of a tree trunk or limb. Or it flattens its body against the tree. Once the hunter has walked past, it scampers to its den and stays there until it feels safe.

Good habitat will produce one gray squirrel per acre. Thus, a square mile of prime woodlands could hold over 600 squirrels. How plentiful gray squirrels are in a given year depends mainly on the previous year's acorn crop. Other foods include walnuts, hickory nuts, pecans, berries and corn.

Gray squirrels begin feeding just before sunrise. They continue for 2 or 3 hours, then retire to their dens. They resume feeding in late afternoon and may remain active until just after sunset. Squirrels move about most on calm, sunny days. Cold or windy weather keeps them denned up. They seldom travel more than 300 yards from their dens.

Mature deciduous forests throughout the eastern United States hold gray squirrels. They favor mixed hardwoods with an abundance of mature oaks, dense undergrowth and few open areas.

GRAY SQUIRRELS have a grayish back and sides, and a whitish or brownish underside. A solid black color phase predominates in some areas. Adults measure 14 to 21 inches from head to tail and weigh ³/₄ to 1¹/₂ pounds.

SIGNS OF SQUIRREL ACTIVITY

•*Acorn shells* at the base of a tree indicate a squirrel den somewhere above. Sign in a large forest is usually left by grays.

•*Stripped corncobs* also reveal squirrel activity. Sign along a fenceline or in a small woodlot is generally that of fox squirrels.

•*Holes* in the snow with leaves and debris around the edge are made by squirrels digging up food caches. Tracks often have clear toe marks.

Fox Squirrels

FOX SQUIRRELS are dull orange on the underside, the tips of the ears and the top of the tail. Some varieties are black or gray. Adults measure 19 to 29 inches from head to tail and weigh 1 to 2¾ pounds.

Named for its reddish, fox-colored fur, the fox squirrel differs from the gray squirrel in behavior and habitat. Some hunters maintain that it is less wary and easier to outwit than the gray.

Fox squirrels spend more time on the ground than grays and rely less on treetops as escape routes. When threatened, they run straight for their dens or hide behind trunks or limbs. Unlike grays, they seldom feed in early morning. They are more active during midday and stray farther from their dens. Fox squirrels can often be seen lying on a limb basking in the sun.

Many hunters refer to fox squirrels as red squirrels. But the true red squirrel is much smaller and is not considered a game animal.

Fox squirrels prefer woodlots, farm groves and strips of timber rather than forests. Like grays, they eat acorns and other nuts. In agricultural areas, corn and other crops make up a high percentage of the diet. Squirrels get most of their water from their food.

Both gray and fox squirrels make a variety of calls. A series of rapid *cherks*, or barks, serves as a warning signal to other squirrels. The familiar chatter means squirrels are approaching one another. A low-pitched chuckle signifies contentment.

MORE SIGNS OF SQUIRREL ACTIVITY

•*Dens* are made by squirrels gnawing at small openings like woodpecker holes. Dens are about 4 inches wide and at least 10 feet off the ground.

•*Hickory trees* produce nuts which draw squirrels. You can easily identify hickories in early fall; they turn yellow earlier than other trees.

•*Nests* consist of twigs and leaves piled into a crotch or woven into the branches. Nests are 1 to 2 feet across, and 20 feet or more above ground.

Hunting for Squirrels

Squirrel activity and movement center around feeding and mating. The most successful hunters know the type and availability of the squirrel's food supply, adjusting their hunting location accordingly. They also know when the breeding season has begun.

Mast crops vary from year to year and squirrels will locate near this food. During late summer squirrels eat wild cherries, poplar buds, maple seeds, mulberries, gum berries and fruits or the seeds of trees that ripen early.

As fall progresses they start their heaviest feeding of the year, preparing for winter. They *cut* or feed on the nuts of pecan, hickory, walnut, oak or beech trees. Piles of small pieces of chewed nut hulls dropped on the ground under these trees, called cuttings, are evidence of feeding.

In agricultural areas, squirrels may concentrate near cornfields; look for sign where squirrels have climbed cornstalks to eat the kernels off the cob or where they have pulled the cobs down.

During the warm parts of early and mid-fall squirrels may start feeding at night and continue until after daylight, resting during the warm part of the day and feeding again in late evening. Feeding and storing nuts for winter lasts longer into the daylight hours as the season progresses. Later in the season squirrels spend more time on the ground gathering, digging and storing nuts.

Hunting can be good during the squirrel's major breeding period, which starts in December or January. Squirrels lose their normal caution as they begin courtship, paying less attention to hunters.

Still-hunting is very productive providing you can move through the woods quietly. Soft-soled shoes and camouflage will help you escape detection. Move slowly, listening and watching for any movement; freeze and investigate each sound. Windy or rainy weather covers your sound, allowing you to move through the woods with less caution.

Stand-hunting can be the most productive tactic when the woods are too noisy to still-hunt. Sit quietly in a feeding area, glassing trees with binoculars, or use a squirrel call to coax squirrels into revealing themselves. Choose a spot with the sun at your back. That way, you can see squirrels but they may not see you. Remain still after shooting one; sometimes squirrels resume normal activity after a few minutes.

Most squirrel hunters use .22 rifles with scopes up to 4x, or 12 or 20 gauge shotguns with No. 6 shot.

SQUIRREL HUNTING TIPS

•*Team-hunt* with a companion. Hiding on the opposite side of a tree trunk is the squirrel's favorite method of eluding the hunter. No matter where the hunter is, the squirrel will always be on the other side of the tree. With this method, however, squirrels cannot hide on the opposite side of a tree without being seen. Be ready to shoot the moment a squirrel moves to your side of the tree.

•*Toss* a stick or rock to the opposite side of a tree. Or tie a string to a bush on one side of the tree, then move to the other side and tug it sharply. The motion will frighten squirrels to your side.

•*Float-hunt* along streams bordered by nut trees. The extra sunlight and moisture result in good nut crops that attract squirrels.

•*Follow* your dog until it trees a squirrel. Then try to maneuver into position for a shot. A barking dog may scare the squirrel to your side.

Raccoons

Many people think of raccoons as mischievous, playful animals. But in reality, adult raccoons are ferocious fighters. They have needle-sharp teeth and can kill or maim hunting dogs twice their size.

Hardwood forests near water make good raccoon habitat. They also live in marshy lowlands, and can adapt to habitats ranging from the Florida mangroves to the arid plains of New Mexico.

Raccoons eat almost any kind of food including berries, fruits, nuts, frogs, crayfish and insects. Sweet corn is a favorite. They hold their food with small, nimble paws that closely resemble human hands.

An adult raccoon may travel up to 5 miles on its nightly feeding rounds, especially in warm weather. During the day they often den up in hollow trees. But they may bed in the tall vegetation along the edge of a marsh, in a culvert or in the ground burrow of another animal. Raccoons frequently use different dens or beds on successive days. They den up for a period after heavy snow; in cold climates they may hibernate.

Ranked among the most intelligent game animals, raccoons also have excellent hearing and good eyesight. They can run up to 15 miles per hour and are good swimmers.

The vast majority of raccoon hunting is done with hounds, especially Walkers, black-and-tans and redbones. Typically, hunters release the hounds and allow them to range ahead to pick up raccoon scent. To better control the hounds, some hunters keep them on leash until the dogs detect fresh scent, then turn them loose. Tracking is easiest on damp, cool nights with a slight breeze.

Hunters listen for the hounds to start baying, then follow the sound. Some hunters use orange or red headlamps to find their way through the woods. The colored light is less noticeable to a raccoon than a white light.

Raccoon hunters continue to follow the dogs until they

RACCOONS have a black, mask-like band across the eyes and black rings on the tail. Most raccoons weigh between 15 and 20 pounds. The largest on record, 62 pounds, 6 ounces, was shot in Wisconsin in 1950.

either tree the raccoon or lose it. Sometimes the chase goes on for miles. Hunters can tell when their dogs tree a raccoon, because the baying becomes more intense.

When pursued by hounds, a raccoon usually runs in large circles, crawling in and out of holes and climbing up and down trees to lose the dogs. It may jump to the ground from as high as 50 feet and scurry away unharmed. It will stay in a tree only when the hounds get so close that other avenues of escape are impossible.

Early in the season you may be able to call raccoons. After dark, take a stand along a streambank, lakeshore, or cornfield. Use tapes or calls to imitate an injured bird or rabbit.

During the day you can often pinpoint those areas that raccoons will frequent during the night. To discover these hotspots, search for holes in trees that could be den sites, or find raccoon tracks in the soft dirt around ponds, marshes or streams. Raccoons go to water to drink and to find foods like crayfish, frogs and small fish. Set up near these areas after dark and simply wait for the raccoons to show themselves.

The majority of raccoon hunters use .22 rifles, although some prefer 20 gauge shotguns with No. 6 or 7½ shot. Where legal, a few hunters use small-caliber pistols.

Hunting Upland Game Birds

A big rooster pheasant bursting from cover would appear to be an easy target. But as every upland bird hunter knows, an unexpected flush will test the skill and composure of even the best wing-shooter.

The term *upland* means high ground. But upland birds can also be found in and around lowlands. Pheasants frequent marsh edges and sharp-tailed grouse often live in bogs. Migratory upland birds also congregate in lowland areas. Woodcock feed along moist streambanks and mourning doves gather near water holes.

All upland birds have keen eyesight and sharp hearing. They have a poorly developed sense of smell, if they can detect odors at all. It pays to approach upland birds quietly and inconspicuously.

The meat of upland game birds varies greatly in color and flavor. The dark breast meat of woodcock and sharptails is laced with blood vessels that supply the muscles with oxygen, enabling the birds to fly long distances. Birds with white breast meat, like ruffed grouse and wild turkey, have fewer blood vessels and cannot fly as far.

Upland bird hunters need little equipment other than waterproof boots and a thorn-proof jacket and pants. If hunting in dense woods or brush, you may need protective glasses.

With the exception of the small-caliber rifles used for wild turkey, upland bird hunters almost always use shotguns. The choke and shot size varies with the size of the bird and the usual shooting distance.

Ring-Necked Pheasants

Every pheasant hunter has been mystified upon arriving at the spot where he saw a rooster land, only to find no trace of the bird.

This Chinese import deserves its reputation as one of the most wily and elusive upland game birds. Its first instinct is to run rather than fly. And despite its large size and gaudy colors, a rooster can slink away unnoticed in ankle-high cover. Sometimes a bird will sit tight, refusing to budge unless you actually step on it.

Pheasants rely on excellent eyesight and good hearing to elude hunters. They can detect ground vibrations not recognizable to humans. These vibrations often cause roosters to crow.

Ringnecks thrive in fertile agricultural areas with good nesting and wintering cover. In spring, they nest in moderately dense cover like hay meadows, clover fields and roadside ditches. They continue to use these areas as roosting sites into the fall, but also roost in weedy cropfields, short slough grass, willow patches and woodlots. They occasionally roost in trees.

Pheasants need heavier cover to escape winter storms.

Primary foods include grain crops like corn, wheat, milo and soybeans. The birds also eat weed seeds and insects. They pick up grit in fields and along roads. This helps their gizzard to grind food.

From June through August, hen pheasants remain with their broods of four to eight chicks. By fall, the chicks begin to mature and the groups break up. As winter approaches, pheasants often flock together where they can find food and heavy cover. Flocks may contain hundreds of birds.

Despite the fact that pheasants are among the hardiest of

RINGNECKS get their name from the white ring around the rooster's neck. Both sexes have brownish tails with black crossbars. The rooster has a reddish-copper breast and a powder-blue rump. Its head has shades of metallic blue, green and purple with a bright red eye patch. The hen (inset) is tan with dark flecks and creamy mottling.

game birds, their average life-span is only 9 months. Normally, only 30 percent of the birds survive from one year to the next, even where there is no hunting season.

In most states and provinces, only roosters are legal game. Pheasants are *polygamous,* meaning that one rooster can mate with many hens. Research has proven that hunters can harvest up to 90 percent of the roosters without affecting the next year's hatch.

Hunters can quickly distinguish the colorful rooster from the drab hen. In addition, roosters often cackle on take-off, removing any doubt about the bird's sex. The typical rooster measures 30 to 36 inches from head to tail and weighs 2½ to 3 pounds. The hen has a much shorter tail and weighs about one-half pound less.

Roosters have spurs on the lower part of the leg. The spurs grow longer and sharper as the bird gets older, reaching ³/4-inch on 3-year-old birds. They use their spurs in spring territorial battles. The sharp spurs on an old rooster can badly scratch a hunter or a dog.

When a rooster bursts from cover, it quickly reaches a speed of 35 to 40 miles per hour. It may fly up to 1 mile, but usually only a few hundred yards. A bird generally spends its entire life in an area of 1/2 square mile or less, leaving that area only if food or cover becomes inadequate.

TYPICAL PHEASANT HABITAT

•*Fertile croplands* offer a good food supply. But expanses of corn and other row crops with little cover support few pheasants.

•*Nesting cover* is vital to pheasants. Hens need grassy cover at least 12 inches high which remains unmowed until after nesting.

•*Winter cover* includes cattail sloughs, thick brush or willows, and woodlots. With good cover, pheasants can survive to -50°F.

Pheasant Hunting Strategies

The pheasant hunting season can be split into two parts: the first few days and the rest of the season. Young pheasants lack the wariness of birds hatched the previous year, so the early days of the season usually offer the easiest hunting. But once the easier birds are gone, you will find it much more difficult to outwit the remaining roosters.

EARLY SEASON. You can locate a good area before the season opens by driving through the countryside and looking for pheasants. The best time to spot the birds is around sunrise on a clear, calm day with dew on the grass. You may also see pheasants in late afternoon. Another way to locate a good hunting area is to look for abundant nesting cover. Chances are there will be birds in the vicinity. If you find a promising location, ask the farmer if you can return to hunt once the season begins.

Early-season hunters often find most of the land covered with crops. In this situation, pheasants may be almost anywhere. To flush birds from large crop or stubble fields, hunters conduct drives. With this much cover still standing, other techniques may not be as productive.

PHEASANT LOCATIONS change as the day progresses. In early morning, look for ringnecks in roosting areas like cattail sloughs, roadside ditches and drainage ditches with grassy cover, and woodlots. By mid-morning, most birds begin feeding in agricultural fields. In early afternoon, look for them in loafing cover like thick grass around the edge of a cornfield. In late afternoon, they return to roosting sites.

Ringnecks usually flush close in early season, so a shotgun with an improved cylinder or modified choke works best. Use shot no larger than No. 6.

LATE SEASON. Once farmers harvest their crops, the birds have fewer places to hide. But birds that survive to late season have learned to evade danger and will often flush far ahead of approaching hunters. Or they will hold extremely tight and let hunters walk past.

In late season, roosters hole up in much heavier cover than they did earlier in the year. They prefer areas with tall trees or other cover that will break the wind. Look for them in brushy woodlots, thick fencelines and drainage ditches lined with slough grass. A favorite hiding spot is a fringe of cattails around the edge of a shallow wetland. Although it prefers heavy cover, a late-season rooster will sometimes seek refuge in a patch of grass not much larger than his body. After a snowfall, hunters often find pheasants under clumps of grass covered with snow. The birds evidently allow themselves to become snowed in.

To bag late-season roosters, one hunter blocks a possible escape route while another approaches from the opposite end of cover. If a rooster flushes too far ahead of the walking hunter, the blocker may get a shot.

For long-range shooting in late season, use a modified or full choke shotgun with No. 4 to 6 shot.

Hunting Pheasants with a Dog

Statistics show that hunters who use dogs bag twice as many ringnecks as those who do not. Most hunters agree that flushers and retrievers work best in heavy cover. Preferred breeds include springer spaniels and Labrador retrievers. Some hunters prefer pointing dogs for large expanses of light, grassy cover, but a wily rooster will often run rather than hold to a point.

A dog with good retrieving skills will seldom lose a crippled ringneck. Pheasants are notoriously difficult to kill. A wounded rooster will usually run off and burrow under heavy grass or brush, where a hunter without a dog would have practically no chance of finding it. A good dog will mark the bird down and relentlessly pursue it through even the thickest tangle of vegetation.

Skilled handlers refuse to work their dogs in standing cornfields or fields of other tall row crops. To a ringneck, an open row is an invitation to run. And most dogs will follow, often disappearing into the field and flushing birds at the opposite end.

A novice pheasant hunter tends to over-command his dog, continually directing it to hunt likely-looking spots. Instead, let the dog use its nose to decide where to hunt. Allow it to range back and forth across cover until it finds fresh scent.

TIPS FOR HUNTING WITH A DOG

•*Hunt* strip-cover with your dog on the downwind side. When the dog detects fresh scent, it will move into the cover and flush or point the bird. Late in the season, another hunter should post at the end of the strip.

•*Follow* your dog through a large expanse of cover. A flushing dog may run when it picks up a scent. You must keep up so birds do not flush out of range. With pointing breeds, you do not have to stay as close.

•*Send* your dog into a thick patch of cover to save you time and energy. Keep track of its location by watching and listening for moving grass or brush. Or attach a bell to the dog's collar.

Hunting Alone for Pheasants

A ringneck's inclination to run rather than fly makes it one of the most difficult birds to hunt by yourself. But you can greatly improve your odds by choosing the right type of spot and by using proven one-hunter techniques.

You are most likely to flush pheasants from small, isolated pieces of cover, such as a patch of short slough grass surrounded by a plowed field. In a large block of heavy cover, a rooster can easily give you the slip. Try to push the birds toward a spot where the cover suddenly ends. Pheasants are reluctant to run into an open field and will usually flush near the edge.

To hunt railroad tracks, road ditches, drainage ditches or parallel windbreaks, work down one side of the strip cover and back on the opposite side. In tall rowcrops, walk crosswise through the rows. This way, you can peer down one row at a time to surprise the birds.

If you walk steadily in a straight line, pheasants will probably sit tight and let you pass. But if you follow a zig-zag path, walking a few steps, then stopping for a moment, nearby pheasants generally become nervous and fly.

Watch and listen carefully for any indication of pheasant movement. If the cover is not too thick, you might catch a glimpse of a rooster running ahead. On a still day, you may hear the slight rustling of a rooster sneaking through the grass.

A fresh snow makes hunting alone much easier. Simply follow fresh pheasant tracks in the snow. Rooster tracks are slightly larger and farther apart than those of a hen. Often the tracks will end at a snow-covered clump of grass. You may have to kick the clump to flush the bird.

Driving for Pheasants

Driving takes advantage of the ringneck's habit of running at the sight or sound of humans. A row of hunters moves through all or part of a large block of cover, while posters wait quietly at the end.

Drivers may flush some pheasants, but more often the birds run to the end of the field. When the drivers approach the posters, the birds realize they are trapped and explode from cover.

If the field is too wide to cover in one pass, the posters can take a vehicle to the end they are blocking. The drivers can take the vehicle back to the opposite end, then make another drive. Or the posters can return, while the drivers start another pass from the end where they finished.

When driving cover that narrows toward one end, start from the widest end. This way you will push the birds into a smaller area, increasing the likelihood of someone getting a shot.

It's best to drive pheasants from the heaviest cover to the lightest. Pushing birds into sparse vegetation forces them to fly. If you drive from light to heavy cover, the birds are more likely to find a safe hiding spot.

You should also try to avoid driving into the sun, especially when it is low in the sky. The glare may blind you or prevent you from distinguishing a rooster from a hen. If you must hunt into the sun, listen for a cackle or look for a long tail.

TIPS FOR PHEASANT HUNTING

•*Choose* dirty cropfields when hunting ringnecks. The weeds provide cover and food that is lacking in clean, well-manicured fields.

•*Leapfrog* stretches of cover. Drop off a partner, drive ahead, then start walking. He walks to the car, drives ahead of you, then resumes walking.

•*Look* for the tallest, thickest cover, especially in cold or windy weather. Trees or tall weeds offer better shelter than the surrounding lower cover.

Bobwhite Quail

BOBWHITE QUAIL roost on the ground. During cool weather, they form a roosting ring, huddling in a plate-sized circle with their tails pointing toward the center. This tactic preserves body heat. Bobwhites prefer a roosting site with plenty of open space above them, enabling them to flush quickly should the need arise. Roosts generally have a south or west exposure, so the ground stays warm in late afternoon.

A covey of bobwhites exploding from cover can rattle even the veteran hunter. Often, each bird flies in a different direction. In the confusion, the hunter may shoot hurriedly without touching a feather.

Despite their stubby wings, quail can fly up to 30 miles per hour and change direction instantly as they dodge through cover. But they usually fly less than 200 yards. Bobwhites are also excellent runners; in fact, they seldom fly unless threatened.

When alarmed, a member of the covey emits a barely audible signal which tells the others to freeze. They squat and remain motionless, relying on camouflage to conceal themselves until the threat passes. If they feel too conspicuous, they scurry to another hiding spot.

Cocks have a white throat patch and a white line through the eye. On hens, the throat patch and line are buff-colored. Bobwhites measure about 10 inches long and weigh 6 to 8 ounces.

Unlike pheasants, bobwhites are *monogamous*, meaning that a cock breeds with only one hen. Quail eggs hatch from May to early July. The cock helps incubate the eggs and raise the chicks. By the start of hunting season, the chicks resemble the adults and the covey consists of 10 to 15 birds.

The birds thrive in areas with a mixture of grasslands, woodlands and brush adjacent to croplands. They use grasslands mainly for nesting; woodlands and brush provide roosting and escape cover. Bobwhites cannot survive in a climate with prolonged periods of deep snow or severe cold. They are unable to dig through deep snow to find food, and their small bodies will not retain enough heat.

Nearly all bobwhites live within 50 to 100 feet of field borders. Seldom will they be found in the middle of a cropfield or woods.

The bobwhite's diet consists mainly of weed seeds, but they also eat insects, acorns and crops like corn, soybeans, wheat and milo. On hot, clear days, the birds feed in early morning and late afternoon. In midday, they take periodic dust baths along sunny field edges. But during cool, damp weather, bobwhites often stay in their roosts until mid-morning, feed intermittently until dark, then return to their roosts.

Each year, predators, severe weather and hunting take a

LOOK *for bobwhite quail in an area that offers ample food and good roosting, escape and nesting cover. The birds feed in harvested crop-fields and along weedy field borders. They find roosting and escape cover along wooded stream courses, woodlot edges, grassy drainage ditches, brushy fencelines and in tall weeds around abandoned buildings. They nest in fields of sedge grass and old pastures.*

heavy toll on the bobwhite population. On the average, a bird lives about 8½ months; only 15 to 20 percent survive to the next breeding season.

TIPS FOR FINDING BOBWHITE QUAIL

•*Osage orange* means good quail cover. Its sharp spines prevent cattle from eating the underbrush. Look for the large, yellow fruits.

•*Giant ragweed* provides roosting and escape cover. The plants stand up to 12 feet tall. Ragweed seeds may be a major source of food in fall.

•*Lespedeza,* or Japan clover, produces seeds which quail eat in winter. Found mainly in the South, it is planted for erosion control.

Hunting for Bobwhite Quail

To many bobwhite hunters, the biggest thrill comes from watching good pointing dogs in action.

A lone hunter who works the cover slowly and thoroughly can kick up some bobwhites by himself. But if the birds decide to hold tight, hunting can be extremely difficult without a dog.

Most hunters prefer English pointers or English setters for large expanses of cover. Brittanys and German shorthairs also work well, but do not cover quite as much ground. Handlers allow the dogs to range far ahead of the hunting party. When a dog detects fresh scent, it locks on point. The covey freezes, giving the hunters plenty of time to move into position.

Most of the birds burst from cover in unison. After the initial flush, work the area a little longer because a straggler or two may remain. Flushing the last birds is often more difficult.

Quail usually fly only a short distance, so you can flush them again. Sometimes the covey stays together, sometimes it breaks up. Watch carefully because the birds may veer off to the side just before they land.

Early season offers the best bobwhite hunting. Coveys consist mainly of young birds that have never been hunted. But as the season progresses, quail become much more unpredictable. Some birds will flush when you slam your car door. Others will run rather than hold to a point. Flushed birds will fly two or three times farther than they did in early season.

Finding downed quail can be difficult, even with a good dog. Some hunters maintain that the scent *washes off* as the birds fly. On the ground, bobwhites compress their feathers so little scent can escape. Bird dogs may walk within inches of wounded quail without finding them. Because of their small size and excellent camouflage, quail can hide in the lightest cover.

Many quail hunters prefer 20 gauge, double-barreled shotguns with improved cylinder and modified chokes. Small shot, usually No. 7½ or 8, works best. Regardless of your shotgun and load choice, pick a single bird and concentrate on that shot. Resist the tendency to *flock shoot*. A wild shot at the covey rarely brings down a bird. You'll also need to learn to judge your effective shooting distance. Because bobwhites are so small, they are probably closer than you think.

BOBWHITE HUNTING BASICS

•*Listen* for the typical *bob-bob-white* whistle during the mating period. You will find birds in the same area once the hunting season opens.

•*Look* for a circle of droppings to pinpoint bobwhite roosting sites. The birds often roost in the same spot for several consecutive nights.

•*Hunt* for bobwhites by yourself using the walk-and-wait technique (page 69). Avoid large blocks of cover. Instead, work brush piles, field corners, narrow strips or other small areas where the birds are easier to find.

•*Flush* a covey by walking toward the birds. If you're hunting in a group, spread apart to increase the chances of getting a shot and to prevent shooting toward each other.

•*Follow* your pointing dogs using a 4-wheel drive vehicle or a mule-drawn quail wagon, or on horseback. This technique enables you to cover more territory than you could on foot.

•*Wear* snakeproof chaps or leggings to protect yourself from snakebites. They will also protect your legs from tough thorns and briers.

California Quail

CALIFORNIA QUAIL have a scaled breast, grayish brown flanks with white streaks, and a teardrop-shaped plume. Males (left) have a black throat with a white border, and a chestnut patch on the belly. Females are less boldly marked. California quail weigh 6 to 7 ounces.

California quail, also called *valley quail,* prefer semi-arid desert brushlands. They feed on the seeds of weeds and brush, and roost in dense patches of tall shrubs or low trees. The birds need water each day and are seldom far from streams, springs or water holes.

In fall, they form large packs numbering from 50 to over 100 birds. They prefer to run rather than fly. When flushed, they usually go only a short distance, then land in bushes or trees.

A good pointing dog can pin down an entire pack by circling the birds. If they fly, watch where they land. They hold tighter on the second flush.

Ideal shotguns for quail are 12 or 20 gauge double barrels with modified and improved cylinder chokes. These guns give you an open pattern for birds that hold and a tight pattern for those that flush at long range. Most hunters use No. 7½ shot.

Gambel's Quail

GAMBEL'S QUAIL resemble California quail, but their buff-white belly is not scaled, and the cap and flanks on the male (right) are reddish-brown. Males also have a black patch on the lower part of the breast. Gambel's quail weigh 5½ to 6½ ounces.

Sometimes called *desert quail*, Gambel's quail are usually found along brushy slopes and in river valleys of arid and semi-arid deserts. They roost in dense thickets or trees, and feed on the seeds of weeds and brush. Normally the birds get enough water from their foods and the dew. But during dry conditions, they rely on a watering site.

The birds come out to feed early and late. They spend the rest of the day in brushy cover to escape the heat. In cool weather, they leave their roosts earlier and may remain in the open all day.

If you approach Gambel's quail in the open, they will probably run before you can get a shot. But if you wait until they move to cover, the birds are more likely to hold. A good pointing dog will improve your odds.

Poisonous snakes are rarely a problem, but some hunters wear leather or plastic leggings.

Mountain Quail

MOUNTAIN QUAIL have a grayish-brown back, a chestnut throat, and chestnut flank with heavy white bars. The head and breast are bluish-gray. Two long, dark feathers form the plume. The sexes look alike. Mountain quail weigh 8 to 9 ounces.

Few upland game birds are as difficult to hunt as mountain quail. They will run at the sight of a hunter, and even a good pointing dog has difficulty pinning them down.

Found at elevations of 2,000 to 10,000 feet, mountain quail live along brushy edges of conifer forests or along brush-lined streams. They eat berries, clover, wild oats and seeds of weeds and grasses; the birds roost under heavy brush or in small conifers. They roam over large areas, retreating to lower elevations in late fall to avoid severe weather.

Coveys generally number only seven to nine birds. They do not form packs, but hunters sometimes see loose groups of birds feeding in the same area.

A flusher or retriever is usually more thorough than a pointing dog and more likely to find single birds that sit tight. Field boots will prevent your dog from injuring its feet on sharp rocks and cactus spines.

Scaled Quail

SCALED QUAIL have breast feathers with dark margins, giving them a scaled appearance. The breast is bluish-gray; the head grayish-brown with a distinctive white-tipped crest. The crest is larger on males (right). Scaled quail weigh 6 to 7 ounces.

Some hunters refer to scaled quail as *blue quail;* others call them *blue racers.* These birds are even more likely to run than mountain quail.

Scaled quail live in semi-arid desert grasslands and in grassy brushlands. They prefer weed and brush seeds for food. The birds roost in dense clumps of brush, grass or weeds. Their water requirements are similar to those of Gambel's quail. In some states, conservation agencies have installed watering devices, helping both quail species to survive during dry periods.

Hunters debate the value of a dog. Some maintain that dogs will flush scaled quail too far ahead, and that they are not needed to find downed birds on the open ground.

If you spot a covey, rush the birds to startle them into flying. Even if you are out of range, shoot to scatter the birds and scare up stragglers. Then hunt the singles, because they will be more likely to hold.

Ruffed Grouse

RUFFED GROUSE have a broad, black or dark brown band on the tail. The band is unbroken on most males but broken on the center two feathers on females (above). There are two color phases, red and gray. Red-phase birds are more common in the South and at low altitudes; grays predominate in the North and at high altitudes. Grouse measure 17 to 20 inches long. They weigh 16 to 24 ounces, but occasionally reach 2 pounds.

Some hunters maintain that a ruffed grouse will intentionally select a flight path that places a tree directly in the line of fire. Whether intentional or not, the ruffed grouse is a difficult target for even the best wingshooters.

Grouse accelerate rapidly, reaching a speed of 40 miles per hour in seconds. But they seldom fly more than 200 yards. Grouse do not run as fast or as far as most other upland birds. When disturbed, birds of both sexes utter a call that sounds like *pete-pete-pete.*

Many hunters call the birds partridge. But the term is a misnomer. The only true partridge in North America are the chukar and Hungarian (pages 154-157). The name ruffed grouse comes from the *ruff,* a tuft of dark feathers on the neck.

Hardwood forests with small clearings and mixed-age aspen trees make the best ruffed grouse habitat. Aspens provide good nesting cover and a year-round source of food. Grouse also favor birch trees, but will live in many other types of hardwood and conifer-hardwood forests.

Besides aspen buds, leaves and twigs, other foods include berries, fruits, clover, nuts, insects and occasionally corn. On warm, sunny days with little wind, grouse feed most of the morning and again in late afternoon. Cold, snowy or windy weather drives the birds into dense thickets or conifer stands. Grouse usually roost on the ground or in conifer trees, but when snow depth reaches 8 to 10 inches, they often burrow into the snow.

Before the spring breeding season, male grouse begin drumming to advertise themselves to females. A bird stands on a log, braces his body with his tail, then starts beating his wings. The sound resembles that of a one-cylinder gasoline engine starting slowly, then gradually speeding up. Some drumming continues through summer and into fall.

Grouse nest in April or May, producing a brood of eight to ten chicks. By fall, the birds are full grown and the brood scatters. Young grouse usually move at least 1 mile, and some relocate up to 10 miles from the hatching site. Once they establish territories, they move very little the rest of their lives.

Young birds lack the wariness of those that have been pursued by hunters. Often a young grouse will sit on the ground or on a tree limb in full view of a hunter. But the birds gain experience quickly. They learn to flush well ahead, or from behind a tree or patch of dense brush where the hunter has difficulty seeing them. In remote areas, adult grouse are no more wary than young birds.

Throughout much of the North, ruffed grouse populations are cyclical, peaking about every 10 years. Populations in peak years may exceed those in poor years by a ratio of 15 to 1. Biologists do not fully understand these cycles.

SIGNS OF GROUSE ACTIVITY

•*Tracks* are closely spaced and about 2 inches long. A grouse places one foot directly in front of the other, so the tracks form a straight line.

•*Droppings* on a drumming log mean that ruffed grouse are nearby. The brownish or greenish droppings are about 1/4-inch in diameter.

•*Holes* in the snow may be burrow-roosting sites. Burrows have an entrance hole and, if the bird has left, an exit hole.

Hunting for Ruffed Grouse

Every grouse hunter has been frustrated upon hearing a whirr of wings, scanning the dense cover, then spotting a bird just as it disappears from sight.

In early season, you may scare up a dozen grouse for every one you see in time for a shot. Even though the birds generally flush close by, leaves severely limit your range of vision. By the time the leaves fall, grouse have become spookier and tend to get up farther away. But they are much easier to see and seldom flush out of shooting range.

A good dog will improve your grouse hunting success. But a dog is not essential because grouse are easier to flush than pheasants or quail. Most hunters prefer pointing breeds, but flushers and retrievers can also be effective if they work close to the handler. Pointing dogs will pin down grouse, enabling you to get close enough for an unobstructed shot. When you move in to flush the bird, avoid walking into dense cover where shooting would be difficult. Because grouse are so well camouflaged, they can be difficult to find without a good dog.

When hunting without a dog, walk through likely cover and stop frequently. You can sometimes hear the birds nervously clucking before they fly. With two or more hunters, walk on opposite sides of thick patches. One hunter is likely to get a shot when a bird flushes.

If you miss or fail to get off a shot, watch where the bird

lands. A flushed bird will often fly off to a dense thicket or land in a tree. You may be able to approach close enough for a second attempt.

You can improve your success by checking the crop of a freshly-killed bird to find out what it was eating. Then, hunt where these foods are plentiful.

Grouse hunting is usually best on calm, sunny days. It seldom pays to hunt in early morning because the birds are still on their roosts. They begin moving after the woods have dried off.

A short-barreled, 20 gauge shotgun with an improved cylinder choke is an ideal grouse gun. The short barrel makes the gun easy to carry through heavy brush and enables you to swing quickly. Most grouse hunters prefer No. 7½ or 8 shot.

TIPS FOR HUNTING RUFFED GROUSE

•*Plan* your strategy using detailed maps of your hunting locale. State forestry departments may publish fire-control maps that show trails and logging roads.

•*Work* the edges of cover. Grouse spend much of their time feeding on fruits and berries that grow along sunlit borders. If a bird flushes, your chances of getting a clear shot are better than in a thick woods.

•*Walk* along a logging road, powerline cut or other trail through the woods. Trails make for easy walking and the edges produce food that attracts grouse. Try to avoid backtracking along the same path.

•*Attach* a bell to the collar of your pointing dog. This helps you keep track of its location. When the bell stops ringing, the dog is on point.

•*Scan* the trees as you walk. Listen for a short flutter of wings, which means a grouse has hopped up to a branch. Grouse in trees evidently feel safe, often allowing hunters to approach within gun range.

•*Listen* for drumming ruffed grouse while hunting. Although most drumming activity takes place in the spring, some males continue to drum into the fall, revealing their locations to hunters.

Sharp-Tailed Grouse

A novice hunter may mistake a sharptail for a hen pheasant, realizing the error only after the bird sails out of range. The two are about the same size and color, but a sharptail has a short, whitish tail and usually clucks when it flushes.

Sharptails prefer large ungrazed grasslands with numerous pockets of trees and brush for cover, and fields of small grain for food. They favor wheat, oats and barley, but also eat berries, seeds, clover and buds. The birds feed in grain stubble or weed patches in early morning, loaf in wooded or brushy areas in midday, then feed again in late afternoon. Sharptails normally roost on the ground.

In early fall, a flock consists of six to eight birds. Later, many flocks combine to form a large pack which may have over 200 birds. When the birds flush, the flock stays together. They usually fly at least one-half mile, and occasionally a mile or more. But a bird or two may hold, so work the area thoroughly. Sharptails are strong runners and sometimes elude hunters by racing out the end of a field as the hunt begins.

Wide-ranging pointing dogs will quickly cover large fields and open brushlands where the birds are normally found. Without dogs, it is difficult to pin down a flock.

Early-season hunters use 12 or 20 gauge shotguns with improved cylinder or modified chokes, and No. 6 shot. After the birds form packs, they are harder to approach, so a full choke may work better.

Look for sharptails in stubble fields early or late in the day. Carry binoculars to spot the birds, and listen for clucking sounds. In windy or stormy weather, hunt along a brushy ravine, a grassy ditch or the lee side of a hill. All of these spots make good windbreaks. And always check brush patches to find loafing sharptails. Other good loafing spots include shelterbelts and grassy areas around abandoned farms.

SHARPTAILS are named for the two long feathers in the center of the tail. The brownish back and wings are covered with white spots. Males have a patch of yellow skin above each eye. These patches are less visible after the breeding season. The birds weigh up to 2 pounds.

Sage Grouse

 t is difficult to imagine a grouse as large as a Canada goose, but a male sage grouse may measure 30 inches long and weigh 8 pounds.

SAGE GROUSE have a mottled, grayish-brown back, a pale breast and flanks and a black belly. The long, pointed tail feathers fan out in flight. Males (above) have a black patch on the chin and upper neck, and a white V across the throat. Females are much smaller than males.

The birds inhabit open, semi-arid country with large sagebrush flats. Buds, leaves and shoots of sagebrush make up most of their diet. They also eat alfalfa, small grains, grasses, clover and berries. The birds feed along sagebrush edges in early morning. You can also find them near water holes, where they eat green vegetation. They rest in gullies and draws in midday, then feed again starting in mid-afternoon.

Sage grouse flocks number only four to six birds early in the hunting season. Later, many flocks join to form packs similar to those of sharptails. The birds hold well in early season. But if hunted heavily, they soon begin to run ahead or flush wildly.

To find sage grouse, glass from a ridge in early morning. Check open areas and edges of cover. If you spot birds, stalk within gun range, then rush the flock. They cannot get off the ground as quickly as other upland birds, so this tactic enables you to gain yardage for a closer shot.

If you don't spot birds, identify water holes, sagebrush edges and ravines that you could hunt later. Hunt near stock tanks, ponds, irrigation ditches or creeks, especially in dry weather. These spots are best in early morning and just before dark. Sage grouse are seldom more than one-half mile from water. A pointing dog works well in early season. But when the birds start to run, a flusher or retriever is more effective.

Use a 12 gauge with a modified or full choke and No. 6 shot to down sage grouse. Some hunters shoot only smaller birds. The meat of older, larger birds tends to be tough and gamey. Because a high percentage of young grouse are shot early in the season, late-season hunting tends to yield more of the older, gamey-tasting birds.

Chukar Partridge

Chukars rank among the most challenging game birds. They inhabit rugged, mountainous terrain that tests the fitness of any hunter.

Named for its call, the chukar was imported from India in the late 1800s. Populations became established in arid portions of the Northwest. Typical chukar habitat varies from bare rocks to sparse grasslands. Because of the open country, the coveys are easy to see, but difficult to approach. They run uphill at the sight of a hunter. When they flush, they usually fly downhill.

Seeds, grasses, leaves and fruits make up most of the chukar's diet. The coveys, which average about 20 birds, begin feeding in mid-morning. On cool days they may feed through the afternoon. They often cover over a mile on their feeding rounds. In hot weather, chukars spend the middle of the day loafing in the shade of rocky bluffs or near springs and water holes. In windy or stormy weather, they seek depressions or crevices in the rocks.

In summer and early fall, chukars can be found at altitudes up to 11,000 feet. A heavy snowfall will drive them to much lower elevations.

CHUKARS use rocky slopes for roosting and escape cover. The birds have a grayish-brown back, a reddish bill and legs, and a black collar that passes through the eye. Black and chestnut bars cover the flanks. Chukars average about 15 inches long and weigh 18 to 24 ounces.

A 20-gauge modified-choke shotgun chambered for 3-inch shells makes a good chukar gun. It is easy to tote over steep terrain, but has a dense enough shot pattern for wild-flushing birds. Most hunters use No. 6 or 7½ shot.

Most hunters use pointing dogs to help pin down the birds and prevent them from running. When your dog detects fresh scent, move into shooting position quickly because chukars may not hold to a point for long.

After a fresh snowfall you can follow chukar tracks. In addition to providing good tracking conditions, snow makes the birds hold tighter and prevents them from running as fast as they do on bare ground.

Hungarian Partridge

HUNGARIAN PARTRIDGE are technically named gray partridge. Native to Hungary, they have a cinnamon head and chestnut bars on the flanks. Males have a chestnut horseshoe on the breast. The birds weigh about 1 pound and measure 12 to 14 inches long.

In northern agricultural areas, the Hungarian partridge, or *hun*, may be the upland game bird of the future. As more heavy cover falls to the plow, populations of birds like pheasants and quail decline. But hun populations often increase.

Besides agricultural areas, huns live in rolling foothills with ample grass and sagebrush. Hunters normally find the birds in short, light cover. Huns feed mainly on grains like corn, oats, wheat and barley, but also eat weed seeds and green leaves.

Huns begin feeding after most of the dew dries off the grass. They feed until late morning, loaf in a grassy area until mid-afternoon, then resume feeding until dusk. The birds roost in alfalfa fields, grain stubble, short grass or even on plowed ground. They often form roosting rings like those of bobwhite quail. In winter, huns may roost in a depression in the snow, or burrow-roost under the snow.

Coveys normally consist of 10 to 12 birds. Huns do not hold well when first approached. They will sneak ahead of a hunter or dog, then burst from cover in unison. The covey remains together. Early in the season, huns fly only a short distance. As the season progresses, they go farther, sometimes over a half-mile.

If you flush a covey out of shotgun range, watch where it lands, then approach the spot from opposite sides. This prevents the birds from slipping away and assures someone of a shot. You can often flush the same covey again.

Hunt with a close-working retriever or flusher, or use a pointing dog. Flushers and retrievers work best in high cover; wide-ranging pointers will find more birds in sparse grasslands or other open terrain.

Shotguns and shells used for huns are similar to those used for chukars. Some hunters prefer 12 gauge guns with full chokes in late season.

Wild Turkey

The wild turkey (*Meleagris gallopavo*), the largest game bird in North America, is related to pheasants, quail and grouse. It is found throughout the United States, except for Alaska, and in parts of Canada and Mexico. There are five recognized subspecies (page 161), which vary slightly in color and size.

The male wild turkey, called a *tom* or *gobbler*, is a large, robust bird weighing up to 30 pounds and standing as high as 4 feet tall. His body color is brownish black with a metallic, iridescent sheen. The head and neck, nearly bald, vary from white to blue to red. Bright red, fleshy bumps, called *caruncles*, droop from the front and sides of the neck, and a fleshy flap of skin, called a *dewlap*, is attached to the throat and neck. A fingerlike protrusion called a *snood*

CHARACTERISTICS unique to the male wild turkey include: (1) snood, (2) dewlap, (3) caruncles and (4) beard. The female (inset) usually lacks these adornments and is duller in overall color than the male.

hangs over the front of the beak. When the tom is alert, the snood constricts and projects vertically as a fleshy bump at the top rear of the beak. A clump of long, coarse hairs, called a *beard*, protrudes from the front of the tom's breast and may grow as long as 12 inches on older birds. Each leg has a spur on it. These spurs are small and rounded on young birds; long, pointed and usually very sharp on mature birds.

The male is called a gobbler for good reason: his rattling, deep-toned call is one of the most recognizable sounds in all of nature. At mating time, toms gobble with full-volume gusto, attempting to attract hens for breeding. Adult males display for hens by fanning their tail feathers, puffing up their body feathers and dragging their wings as they strut. Their heads and necks turn bright red during breeding season or when the tom is otherwise excited.

WILD TURKEYS have a field of vision of about 300 degrees, thanks in part to eyes mounted on opposite sides of the head.

Adult females, or *hens*, are considerably smaller than toms, rarely weighing more than 10 to 12 pounds. Their overall body color is duller than the male's and lacks his metallic, iridescent sheen. The hen's head and neck are usually blue-gray in color and sparsely covered with small, dark feathers. Caruncles are sometimes present, but smaller than those on toms. Some hens grow small, rudimentary beards and spurs. Although they don't gobble, hens make a variety of cluck, purr, cutt and yelp sounds. Dominant hens may assert themselves with a display resembling that of the male, though they do not strut.

Juvenile birds mature quickly. By their fifth month, the juvenile male *(jake)* and juvenile female *(jenny)* closely resemble adult birds. However, juveniles have darker legs, which turn pink as the birds age. Jakes make feeble gobbles, higher in pitch than the calls of mature toms. Their beards are shorter in length and usually have amber-colored tips.

With its powerful legs, the wild turkey is an exceptional runner, and has been clocked at speeds up to 12 miles per hour. Although strong short-distance fliers, turkeys usually run when threatened. When necessary for escape, turkeys launch themselves with a standing leap or a running start and accelerate to 35 miles per hour in a matter of seconds. They cannot remain in the air for more than a few hundred yards, but can glide for a half mile or more when coasting down from a ridgetop.

SUBSPECIES

Subspecies can be difficult to distinguish from one another, since regional variations within the group can be more dramatic than physical differences between the subspecies.

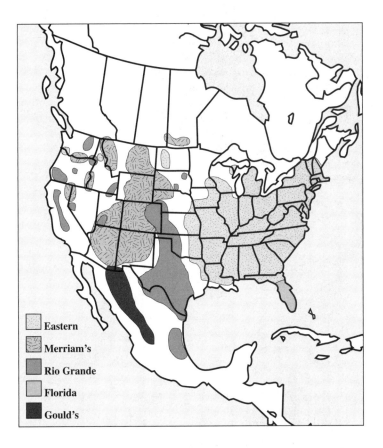

Eastern
Merriam's
Rio Grande
Florida
Gould's

In addition, where the subspecies' ranges overlap, cross-breeding produces hybrid birds that show traits of both parents. A map (above) showing the current range of all five subspecies is a good starting point in determining where subspecies live.

Turkey Calls and Decoys

Turkey calls have been an important part of the hunt ever since man discovered he could talk turkey and the birds would respond. Turkey calls have always been deadly at drawing toms to hunters.

Calling is considered by most devoted turkey hunters to be the only sporting way to take a gobbler. Calling is the

161

PROPER placement of a diaphragm call in your mouth is crucial to success. (1) Use your tongue to position the call against the roof of your mouth with the straight edge facing forward. (2) Position the call so the forward edge nearly touches the back of your front teeth. (3) Place the top of your tongue lightly against the latex reed, and (4) expel short bursts of air between the top of your tongue and the reed, while saying the word "chirp." Stay at it, and you will soon be able to produce acceptable yelps, the first call you should learn. Once you have mastered the yelp, begin practicing other calls.

Proper Diaphragm Call Placement

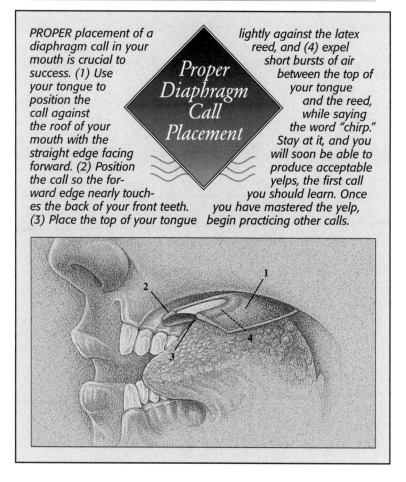

fun part of turkey hunting. Mastering a variety of different calls — learning when to yelp, cluck, purr or cutt, knowing when to call softly and when to crank up the volume — this is the art of spring turkey hunting.

Under the right circumstances, turkeys can be ridiculously easy to call. But don't count on it. When hens are abundant or hunting pressure is heavy, only a hunter who has mastered the art of calling will walk out of the woods with a gobbler slung over a shoulder.

Calls designed to lure gobblers to the hunter can be divided into two broad categories: friction calls and air-activated calls. Although each has its advantages and disadvantages, the friction calls are generally easier to operate. Friction calls include the push-pull call, the box call and the slate-and-peg call. Air-activated calls include the tube call and the diaphragm call.

A third category of calls, locator calls, are used to elicit a response from a turkey without attracting the bird to your position. This response is most commonly referred to as a *shock gobble*. Turkeys have been known to shock gobble to the sound of a squeaking fence, a slamming car door or a bellowing Holstein, and a host of other sudden, loud sounds. Most locator calls imitate animals such as crows, owls, hawks and coyotes, but loud cutting on a turkey call can also prompt a shock gobble.

There are dozens of commercial calls on the market, and while there is no need to buy and use all of them, a hunter is wise to use a variety of calls. Wild turkeys can be fickle, preferring a box call one morning, a diaphragm the next. A well-prepared hunter is ready to switch calls on those mornings when his old standbys just aren't making the grade.

However, as important as calling is, woodsmanship is equally important. In fact, an accomplished woodsman – a hunter intimately familiar with the land and the turkeys that live on it – can take gobblers with amazing consistency without ever touching a call.

DECOYS. A well-positioned turkey decoy is often the final touch needed to lure a shy tom into shooting range. Especially in open country, toms responding to a hen call may grow suspicious if they can't spot the source of the call. But if they see a decoy, the reassured gobblers often commit and waltz into range. A decoy can work wonders on hard-hunted birds, which tend to be leery of even the best calling.

Typically, hunters place two decoys (one hen and one jake) out at a distance of about 20 yards. The decoys should be about 6 feet apart, with the jake a bit closer to the hunter's location than the hen. When a tom spots the pair, he often runs in quickly to scare off the jake and steal the hen. A hunter must have his gun up and ready when he first spots the tom in the distance; it doesn't take the jealous tom but a few seconds to be within easy shotgun range.

Understanding Daily Patterns

To effectively hunt wild turkeys in spring, a hunter must understand the bird's daily movement patterns. Bagging a wild turkey is largely a matter of being in the right place at the right time.

At first light, as turkeys begin to awaken in their roosting trees, toms begin to gobble, while hens utter soft tree yelps. Usually the birds fly to the ground as soon as there is enough light for them to spot predators, but this fly-down can be as late as 2 hours after sunrise if the morning is rainy or foggy. Turkeys roosting in small wood lots in relatively open areas tend to fly down sooner than birds roosting in deep timber, where daylight is longer in arriving.

When a turkey gobbles on the roost in early morning, he is trying to draw a hen to him. If successful, the tom will fly down to join the hen. If a hen doesn't appear, the tom flies down and walks to his strutting area, while continuing to gobble.

Strutting zones are located in open areas where toms can be easily seen by hens, such as a field edge, logging road or pasture. In hill country, strutting areas are often located on elevated ridges, points or hilltops. In flat country, gobblers often strut in semi-open hardwood bottoms.

When the tom arrives at the strutting zone, he continues to gobble until he attracts a hen. Once a hen arrives, however, the gobbler begins to strut and his gobbling becomes infrequent. The tom may attract several hens simultaneously.

A gobbler follows hens as they wander to feed, mating with each several times during the morning, if they permit. Identifying feeding areas can be difficult, since wild turkeys eat such a wide variety of food. In big timber, turkeys often wander along, foraging on whatever they find. In agricultural areas, turkeys feed in crop fields a good deal of the time.

Only in the arid regions of the West and Southwest do turkeys habitually seek water during their daily route. In most regions they obtain sufficient water from dew or in the plants they consume.

By mid- to late morning, after satisfying their hunger, turkeys often treat themselves to a dust bath. Bred hens may then retire to the nest to lay or incubate. Gobblers may rest at this time or resume gobbling and continue to search for new hens.

Midafternoon finds turkeys on the move and feeding once again. During the last hour of day, the flock feeds toward roosting sites. They usually fly up at sunset or shortly thereafter. Birds often change limbs or even roosting trees a number of times before settling in for the night.

Turkey Hunting

The first step in a successful hunt is to find good turkey habitat. Assuming you have scouted adequately, you should know several spots that hold birds.

Ideally, you'll want to "roost" a gobbler on the eve of the hunt, which means you actually see or hear the bird in his roost tree. Return before first light, slip within 100 yards of this roost, sound a couple of tree yelps at dawn, and odds are good the gobbler will fly down practically in your lap.

To "put a bird to bed," set up near a roosting site in early evening. Turkeys feed toward a roost tree in late evening, usually fly into it around sunset and settle in before dark.

If you cannot spot birds, listen for them. Occasionally, toms gobble a time or two after roosting, and hens sometimes yelp. More often, you'll have to make them gobble by using a locator call. Walk through likely habitat, pausing every quarter mile or so to call. If a gobbler responds, move toward him, eliciting additional shock gobbles until you've pinpointed his location. Mark the site and the trail to it with strips of toilet paper or surveyor's tape so you can find your way back before dawn.

As day breaks, give a few quiet tree yelps. Chances are good that the gobbler will reply, but if he doesn't, resist the temptation to call louder or more often. Overcalling while a tom is still on the roost is a common mistake.

If you failed to put a gobbler to bed the night before, plan to be at a good listening position well before first light. Hilltops and ridges are best. On most mornings, toms begin gobbling spontaneously, but if you hear no gobbling by the time there is enough light for you to see individual limbs on trees, then try to elicit a gobble with an owl or crow call. When you hear a gobbler within reasonable distance, try to get within 100 yards before setting up to call him.

Turkeys usually fly from the roost as soon as there is enough light for them to see predators on the ground. However, on rainy, foggy or unseasonably cold mornings, they may stay on the roost for an hour or more after sunrise.

They'll use the same strutting grounds day after day. These are usually in relatively open areas, such as open timber, field edges, pastures or logging roads, where toms can watch for approaching hens and hens can clearly see their strutting displays. Once you find these sites, you can hunt them productively for years, because turkeys return to the same strutting zones season after season.

Hunters often make the mistake of yelping loudly and frequently. Call just enough to let a gobbler know you are there. Every few minutes, scratch the ground to mimic the sound of a foraging turkey. This assures the gobbler that a hen is still nearby, but since she ignores his calling, he sometimes goes against his own instinct and sashays toward her.

The prime early morning strutting/gobbling period may last a few minutes to an hour. Occasionally, a tom will return to his strutting zone in late morning after his original partners abandon him.

Two strategies can produce results after the prime early morning period: run-and-gun, or sit-and-wait.

To use the run-and-gun approach, walk quickly through the area, stopping frequently to blow a locator call. Search for a bird that responds to every call you make. When you find such a bird, get within 200 yards in open country, half that distance in timber; sit down and get ready before you make a single hen call. Call just often enough to keep the bird gobbling, so you know where he is. If the bird continues to gobble in response to your calls, but moves steadily away, determine his direction and attempt to get ahead of him. If he moves steadily in your direction, call sparingly and stay ready.

Picking a good feeding spot and waiting patiently for a flock of hungry birds to arrive is also a good tactic before 10:00 A.M. This sit-and-wait tactic is most successful if you know the area well enough to predict travel routes. A blind can be a real asset when playing this waiting game, as can a decoy or two. Patience is the key. Turkeys feed at midmorning, and a feeding flock is in no hurry, covering only about 200 yards per hour, on average.

Cover lots of territory after 10 A.M. Use locator calls and loud cutting to elicit gobbles. Locator calls are better than hen calls for prompting a tom to begin gobbling. Once you've elicited a shock gobble, set up and get ready to seduce the bird with your most authentic hen calls. If you begin by making hen yelps, a tom may arrive before you are prepared to deliver the proper greeting.

If you prefer to sit and wait for your bird, late morning is a good time to stake out strutting zones. Gobblers that have been deserted by hens frequently meander back to their strutting zones and will readily respond to calls.

Gobblers can still be taken in the afternoon, though it takes patience and a slightly different strategy. Find a turkey hangout — a dusting area or feeding site — set out a decoy or two, relax against a big tree and give a few yelps every 15 minutes or so. If a gobbler comes to your call at this hour, he usually won't announce himself until within shooting range. Many hunters have been jarred from mid-day naps by tiptoeing gobblers shouting at close range.

Action picks up again in late afternoon, when turkeys begin actively feeding and, later, working toward the roost. If you have located a roosting area, determine the most likely direction from which the birds will approach, and set up in their path. If you haven't pinpointed a roosting area, spend the last hour of daylight covering ground and using a locator call. If you hear a gobbler, slip in close and work the bird with hen calls. Even if you don't get a shot, you'll know where to continue the hunt in the morning.

Mourning Doves

MOURNING DOVES have a slate-blue back, a fawn-colored breast with a pinkish cast, and a black spot behind the ear. They measure 11 to 13 inches from head to tail and weigh about 3½ to 5 ounces.

The nation's hunters harvest about 50 million doves annually, more than all other migratory game birds combined. The continent's dove population is estimated at 500 million, making it the most common game bird.

Mourning doves cannot tolerate cold weather. In northern states, the birds begin flying south after the first frost. Prior to migration, they form flocks consisting of several hundred birds.

Doves prefer open fields with scattered trees and woodlots. The birds need water each day, so there must be a pond, stock tank, flooded gravel pit or river nearby. Doves nest in grass, shrubs, stubble fields or trees, especially evergreens.

Nesting begins in early spring and continues through early fall. Doves raise up to four broods, with both parents caring for the young. After predation and weather-related losses, broods average about one bird each. This trait of raising multiple broods is unique among game birds. It assures a relatively stable population from year to year, with or without a hunting season.

Weed seeds form the bulk of the dove's diet. They favor foxtail, doveweed, ragweed and wild hemp. Other foods include corn, soybeans, sunflowers, oats and wheat.

Doves fly to their feeding areas at dawn, feed until mid-morning, then head for water. Through midday, they rest in dead or dying trees near a feeding area, a water hole or a small pond. Doves resume feeding in late afternoon, then return to a watering site late in the day.

At dusk, they fly to their roosts, often to the same trees they used during the day. If not disturbed, doves will continue to use the same roosting and watering areas.

Mourning doves can fly up to 55 miles per hour. Their normal flight is smooth, effortless and direct. But they flare quickly at the sight of hunters, darting and weaving erratically as they fly away.

WHERE TO FIND DOVES

•*Roosting trees* are usually within 2 miles of water. A favorite roosting spot is a sand bar in a river where the birds find dead trees close to water.

•*Water holes* used by doves often have muddy water and bare ground along the edge. The best water holes have trees with dead branches nearby.

•*Idle fields* attract doves because they provide an ample supply of weed seeds. Doves prefer to pick seeds from bare ground. They seldom feed in dense vegetation.

•*Gravel roads* provide grit. Doves pick up sand and small gravel along roads in early morning and late afternoon. They also find grit along streams and in fields.

Hunting for Doves

In a dove-hunting study, observers tallied an average of eight shots for every dove bagged. The bird's elusive flight accounts for this startling statistic.

Most dove hunters simply find a stand along a commonly used flight path. It may be a route between a roosting and feeding site, or between a feeding and watering area. Conceal yourself in a brush patch or near a fenceline or tree, then pass-shoot as the birds fly through.

When selecting a stand, remember that mourning doves often fly near a dead tree, telephone pole or any object taller than the surrounding cover. They frequently fly through a gap in a treeline to reach a feeding area or water hole. Often they skirt the end of a point of cover extending into a feeding field. If stands within gun range of these spots do not produce, watch where the birds are flying and change your location accordingly.

Some hunters set decoys on the ground or in a tree near a water hole. This increases the chance of birds flying over your end of the pond. Hunters also place decoys in trees or on fences near feeding or roosting sites.

Hunting by yourself can be difficult; the birds may land in an open field where they would be nearly impossible to approach. By stationing several hunters around the edge, you can keep the birds moving and improve shooting for everyone.

You can also jump-shoot doves when they are feeding in crop fields or resting in woodlots or thickets. This technique works best during midday when the birds are not flying and pass-shooting is slow.

Hunting is generally best in early season. But after a few days, the birds become much warier and learn to avoid hunters. Hunting success often picks up again as migrant birds move in from the North. Most dove hunters prefer warm, calm days. The birds seldom fly in windy or rainy weather.

Dove shooters need a minimum of equipment. Camouflage clothing is ideal, but any drab outerwear will do. Many hunters use semi-automatic or pump shotguns. The repeating action enables them to keep shooting when doves are flying. A variable or screw-in choke enables you to vary your shot pattern, depending on the range of the birds. An improved cylinder or modified choke with No. 7½ or 8 shot normally works best. But in late season some hunters switch to a full choke and No. 6 shot.

HOW TO PASS-SHOOT FOR DOVES

•*Find* a stand in the shade to reduce your visibility. But avoid any stand where overhead cover restricts your field of fire.

•*Select* a spot where natural cover breaks up your outline. Even though you are not fully concealed, doves will not flare if you remain still.

•*Use* a cooler to carry your hunting gear and to keep the birds on ice during hot weather. The cooler can also be used as a seat.

Woodcock

Hunters who own pointing dogs consider woodcock, or *timberdoodle,* the ideal quarry. Even with a dog inches away, a bird will hold tight, confident in its near-perfect camouflage.

Woodcock have a chunky body with a mottled brownish back and sides, and black bars on top of the head. They measure 10 to 12 inches, weigh 6 to 8 ounces, and have a bill about 2½ inches long.

Eyes on the side of the head give the birds excellent lateral vision. Some researchers believe that woodcock rely on an acute sense of hearing to find worms in the ground. The birds can fly as fast as 30 miles per hour. When flushed, they usually land within 100 yards.

Most woodcock breed in the northern states and Canada. They start their southerly migration in early to mid-October, leaving en masse once the ground freezes or after a heavy snow. Woodcock stop off in the same resting areas each year.

Young forests with trees 10 to 20 feet tall make the best woodcock habitat. The soil should be damp with little grassy cover. Heavy ground cover makes it difficult for the birds to find earthworms, their favorite food.

Woodcock feed mainly around dawn and dusk. Besides earthworms, the birds eat insect larvae, seeds, berries and green leaves. During the day, they rest on the ground, feeding only occasionally. In cool weather, look for them on sunny hillsides or other sunlit areas. On a hot day, they sit in the shade, often below evergreens.

The best woodcock hunting is during the migration period. Northern hunters may get some shooting at resident birds, but when the migration peaks, they may flush up to 30 birds per hour.

Hunters who use dogs flush at least twice as many birds as those who do not. Because woodcock blend in so well with the leaves, downed birds can be difficult to find without a dog.

A short-barreled 20 gauge with an improved cylinder choke is an excellent gun for woodcock. Most hunters use No. 7½ or 8 shot, but some prefer No. 9.

TIPS FOR HUNTING WOODCOCK

•*Look* for woodcock in alder thickets. Alders generally grow in moist soil where woodcock can easily find earthworms. The birds can also be found around willows and young birch trees in damp bottomlands.

•*Find* a good woodcock area by looking for their dried liquid droppings, or *chalk*. The white blotches are about the size of a half dollar.

•*Hunt* for woodcock along a moist streambank, along the edge of a swamp, or wherever you can find rich soil adjacent to water.

•*Shoot* while a woodcock is rising or just before it levels off. Once it begins to fly straight away, it darts and weaves, making a difficult target.

Hunting
Waterfowl

All waterfowl are ideally suited for a life spent in and around water. Webbed feet give them extraordinary swimming ability, and their long necks and broad, flattened bills allow them to feed on aquatic plant and animal life. Waterproof plumage and thick layers of insulating down keep these birds from losing body heat in cold water.

Geese are distinguished mainly by their large size, with some approaching 15 pounds. During the migration, geese may form enormous flocks numbering in the tens of thousands. Geese exhibit no coloration differences between the sexes. They rarely breed before their second year and may live for 25 years. Geese mate for life and maintain stronger family bonds than do ducks, with both parents caring for the young.

Ducks differ from geese in that sexes usually vary in coloration. Males have distinctive, colorful plumage, while females are camouflaged with mottled, drab browns. Pair bonds are temporary, with the drake deserting the female shortly after breeding. Most ducks are short lived, but a few have been known to live 15 years.

Puddle ducks include some of the most widely hunted species. They feed on or just below the surface, either skimming food or tipping up, with feet and rump pointing skyward. Puddle ducks are adept at walking and feeding on land. They can take flight almost instantly by jumping straight into the air.

Diving ducks have legs and feet positioned far back on their bodies. Rather awkward on land, they spend most of their time in the water. They eat more invertebrates and fish than do puddle ducks and feed by diving below the surface. They usually fly in a straight line.

Mergansers are distinguished from the other ducks by their narrow, pointed bill with serrated edges, and their crested heads. Often called fish ducks, they feed primarily on minnows and other small fish.

Sea ducks spend much of their lives on the ocean. Expert divers, they have been known to reach depths of 200 feet to feed on mollusks, crustaceans and fish.

Identification of species and sexes requires a great deal of practice, especially with ducks. But you can recognize the major types of waterfowl by their body size and wingbeat. Geese are larger than ducks and their wingbeat is slower. Puddle ducks have a faster wingbeat, but not as fast as diving ducks.

Covering the biological description and profile of every important duck species is beyond the scope of this book. Please refer to *North American Game Birds* or *Duck Hunting* for a complete biological description of each species.

Puddle Ducks

LEGS positioned near the center of the body give a puddler good balance, so it can easily walk and feed on land.

As their name suggests, these ducks commonly frequent small, shallow bodies of water, but they may also be found on big water. Also called *dabblers,* they feed on or just below the surface, mainly on aquatic vegetation. They may skim food off the water, or they may tip up, submerging their upper body to feed while leaving their feet and rump pointing up. In fall, some puddle ducks also feed in grain fields. Their predominantly vegetable diet explains why they are considered better eating than most other ducks. Large wings give puddle ducks good maneuverability. They will often circle a potential landing site several times, inspecting it closely before setting down. There are a total of 12 puddle duck species that are currently huntable in North America.

COLORED WING PATCHES *are present on most puddlers. Most have a patch, called a* speculum *(arrow) on the wing's trailing edge. The speculum is usually iridescent.*

TIPPING UP, *or dabbling, is the usual puddle duck feeding method.*

Puddle-Duck Hunting

The widespread distribution of puddle ducks, combined with their excellent table quality, accounts for their tremendous popularity among waterfowl hunters.

As a rule, puddle ducks prefer smaller water than diving ducks; even the shallowest slough or tiniest creek may offer top-rate hunting. But puddlers are also found on some of the continent's largest waters, including the Great Lakes and Utah's Great Salt Lake. While divers are comfortable riding out big waves in open water, puddlers are usually found in calm water. In windy weather, they seek shelter along a lee shore.

You don't need a lot of expensive equipment to hunt puddle ducks. Jump-shooting and pass-shooting require nothing more than a shotgun and a few shells, and you can decoy the birds into a small body of water with only a half-dozen decoys. Hunting on big water, however, is much more involved and requires considerably more equipment, including a good-sized boat and a minimum of several dozen decoys.

Mallards are the most numerous of the puddle ducks, and

most other puddler species feel comfortable in their company. Teal, for instance, are commonly seen flying with mallards, and wood ducks often loaf in the same area as mallards. As a result, you can use mallard decoys and calls to attract most any kind of puddle duck.

In setting decoys for puddle ducks, remember that puddlers rest in looser groups than divers, so your decoys can be spread out much more. Some hunters leave as much as 10 feet between individual decoys. Diving-duck hunters seldom leave more than 6 feet.

Calling is of utmost importance in puddle-duck hunting. The birds, by nature, are quite vocal, and they look for reassurance from ducks on the water before making the decision to land. If you are not a competent caller, however, it's better not to call; you'll scare away more birds than you'll attract.

Puddlers are generally considered to be smarter than divers, but this "intelligence" may, in part, be a reflection of their migration and feeding habits. Because they migrate earlier than divers, they're exposed to a longer period of hunting pressure, so they're more likely to recognize the difference between decoys and the real thing.

PUDDLE-DUCK HUNTING TIPS

•*Use* available cover to sneak up on a group of ducks. Be patient and walk quietly to avoid spooking them before you are within range.

•*Use* several goose decoys when hunting puddle ducks in the field. Ducks often feed with geese and the larger decoys will add to the visibility of your spread.

•*Kick water* with your boot when hunting flooded timber. The ripples indicate to circling ducks that others are dabbling in the water.

•*Pass-shoot* from a strip of land between two lakes or between a lake and a grain field. Ducks will choose the route that crosses the least land.

•*Float* a small stream or river using a low-profile duck boat or a canoe. Hug the inside turns as long as possible. Ducks usually rest below the points, and they won't see you coming until the last minute.

PUDDLE-DUCK DECOY SETS

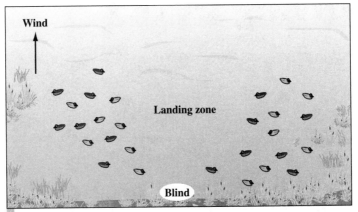

WITH THE WIND AT HUNTERS' BACKS, decoys should be set in two pods with a good-sized landing pocket between the pods. The outermost decoys should be no more than 30 yards from the blind. The blind is positioned so the hunters are facing the pocket. Without a pocket, ducks may land beyond the decoys, out of shooting range.

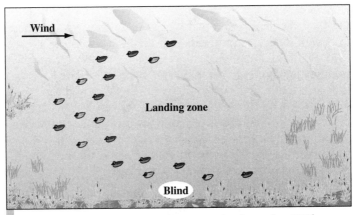

WITH THE WIND FROM THE LEFT, arrange the decoys in a "C" formation to the left of the blind, as shown. Ducks do not like flying over decoys to land; this way, they do not have to. When the wind is from the right, reverse the entire decoy setup.

Diving Ducks

RUNNING on the water helps divers gain enough speed for take-off. Their small wings provide less lift than those of puddlers.

With legs positioned farther back on the body, these ducks are more adept at diving beneath the surface than are puddle ducks. Their feet are larger for their size, so they are better underwater swimmers. The leg position also makes it more difficult for them to walk on land, explaining why they seldom feed in agricultural fields. The diet of most divers consists mainly of invertebrates and fish, explaining their strong taste. But some, such as canvasbacks and redheads, feed heavily on wild celery and other aquatic vegetation, and are considered better eating.

Sea ducks, a subcategory of diving duck, differ from ordinary divers in that they spend most of their life in coastal areas. They have remarkable diving ability, with some species descending to depths of more than 200 feet to feed on mollusks, crustaceans and fish.

Mergansers, often called fish ducks, are also classified as a subcategory of diving duck. They feed even more heavily on fish than other divers, and their serrated bill is ideal for catching and holding small fish until they can be swallowed whole. Their crested head easily distinguishes them from other diving ducks.

There are 19 huntable diving duck species in North America.

FLYING LOW over the water in tight flocks is typical behavior among most diver species. In flight, divers can be distinguished from puddlers by their shorter, faster wingbeat.

LARGE FEET and legs positioned far back on the body account for the diving ability of these ducks.

WHITE to dark gray wing patches are found on most diving duck species.

Diver Hunting

If you're looking for a wingshooting challenge, diving ducks are the perfect quarry. When a flock of divers streaks along a decoy line, it's not uncommon for a hunter to shoot at the lead bird and drop the third or fourth one back.

Due to the divers' preference for big water, hunters need more and different equipment than they ordinarily do for puddle-duck hunting. Instead of a 12- or 14-foot, shallow-draft duck boat, for instance, you'll need a 16- or 18-foot, deep-hulled semi-V to negotiate water that can turn rough in a hurry. You'll also need more decoys than you would for puddle-duck hunting and, possibly, a floating blind.

The divers' habit of forming large open-water rafts, particularly in late season, adds to the hunting challenge. Some hunters use low-profile sneak or sculling boats to approach birds in open water without alarming them.

Because divers migrate much later in the season than puddle ducks, you'll be hunting in considerably colder weather. Warm, waterproof clothing, including insulated boots and gloves, is a requirement.

Crippled divers often attempt to escape by swimming away underwater or with their head at water level. You'll need a determined, hardy retriever, preferably a Labrador or Chesapeake, that is capable of making long retrieves in cold, choppy water.

In puddle-duck hunting, the idea is to lure birds into the decoys and take them when they're "putting on the brakes," meaning that their wings are cupped and they are about to land. In diver hunting, the birds are less likely to slow down, so you'll probably have to take them as they're winging along a line of decoys that leads to your blind.

Instead of shooting at birds that are barely moving, you're attempting to hit birds barreling along at speeds up to 75 miles per hour. To be successful, you must learn the swing-through shooting technique (page 41) and do a lot of practicing to determine the proper lead.

Calling is seldom necessary in diver hunting. The birds spot the decoys from a distance and their curiosity draws them in without any vocal enticement. Nevertheless, many hunters try calling anyway, using a diver call or rolling their tongue against a mallard call to mimic the characteristic diver "purr."

Divers differ from puddlers in that they do not hesitate to land in rough water. As a result, there is no need to set your decoys off a lee shore. It's more important to set them where the birds are feeding, regardless of wind direction.

Yet another difference: divers do most all of their feeding on the water, so the field-hunting techniques that work so well for puddle ducks are not effective for divers. Practically all diver hunting is done on the water or on passes between two bodies of water.

Diver hunting is not for everyone. Not only does it require a high tolerance for inclement weather, it can be a lot of work. But if you're a hardy soul who loves the whistle of wings, there's no more exciting shooting.

TYPES OF DIVER DECOY SPREADS

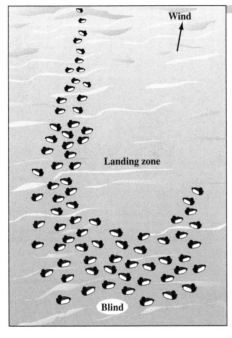

Wind

Landing zone

Blind

THE J-HOOK. This setup works well off a point or in open water. The long tail extends well beyond shooting range. The largest clump of decoys is placed at the hook of the "J," which forms a landing zone.

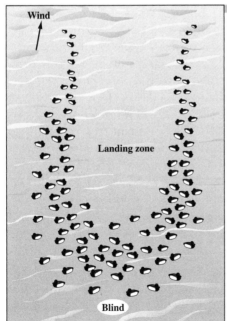

Wind

Landing zone

Blind

THE V-FORMATION. This setup is similar to the J-hook, but it has two tails extending out into the water, rather than one, giving the birds an additional option for approaching the blind.

Geese

CANADA GEESE have a black head with a white chin bar. The back is grayish or brownish, and the belly is whitish. Biologists recognize over 12 varieties of Canada geese, the largest being the giant Canada; the smallest, the cackling goose.

The goose is an extremely family-oriented bird. Flocks consist of one or two family units, each numbering between four and six birds. As the migration progresses, many flocks join to form large concentrations, which may number in the thousands. Geese will often fly in a very distinct V-formation with a much slower wing-beat than ducks. Large, powerful wings enable geese to take flight very quickly, even though some Canada geese reach a weight of 15 pounds.

An exceptional homing instinct draws geese to the same waters every year. And they often return to the same feeding areas on consecutive days. If the food supply holds up, they will come back to the exact spot in the field.

The fall diet of geese consists of waste grain, green plants such as clover, grasses and new shoots of wheat and oats. Geese feed in open fields where they can easily see in all directions.

About three out of four bagged geese are juveniles, but some live 25 years. To survive that long, they must learn to be extremely cautious. Old birds scrutinize a landing site and veer off immediately if anything looks suspicious.

SNOW GEESE are pure white with black wing tips. Two subspecies are recognized: the greater snow goose and the lesser snow goose. Lesser snow geese may sport either dark or white plumage; dark-phase birds are called blues.

ROSS' GEESE resemble the lesser snow goose, but are smaller and have a stubbier bill. Ross' geese often travel with snow geese and can easily be identified in flight by their faster wingbeat.

WHITE-FRONTED GEESE, also called speckle bellies, have a brownish head, neck and back. The undersides are whitish with dark brown speckles. A distinctive white facial patch rings the base of the pinkish bill.

BRANT GEESE, both Atlantic and Pacific (inset), can be recognized in flight by their rapid wingbeat. The head, neck and chest are black, and the sides of the neck are marked with white streaks. The Pacific brant has a darker underside and more pronounced neck marks.

Hunting Geese

For many hunters the thrill of goose hunting comes from watching thousands of geese fly out to feed and listening to their piercing clamor.

Hunters accustomed to shooting ducks often have trouble hitting geese. Because the birds are so large, the tendency is to underestimate their distance and speed. Goose hunters use 12 or 10 gauge shotguns with modified or full chokes. Shot sizes range from No. 3 to T shot.

Hunting with decoys can be done both in feeding fields and on the water. When hunting in a field, you will often need a large number of decoys to attract the birds in for a look. Typically, hunters locate geese in midmorning or late afternoon by scouting grain fields near resting waters. After securing permission, these hunters then set up decoys in the field before the next feeding period.

When hunting for Canada or white-fronted geese in the early season, set your decoys in small clusters to imitate a small family group. Fewer decoys are often required early in the season because the geese haven't grouped up for the fall migration.

When hunting snow or Ross' geese, some hunters have been known to use well over a thousand decoys in order to successfully decoy the most cautious goose of North America. Combining large shell decoys and silhouette decoys, hunters will mix in Texas Rag decoys, white garbage bags and wind-sock-style decoys to increase the mass and visibility of the spread. Hunters rarely hunt snows on the water with decoys.

Brants can also be hunted with decoys, most commonly on the water. Setting two separate groups of decoys and leaving a place for the geese to land in the middle is the most common setup.

Most pass-shooting takes place in areas surrounding goose refuges or other waters with large concentrations of birds. Flight paths to and from a lake vary, depending on wind direction and the location of the feeding field being used. To select a good pass-shooting spot, spend a few hours watching the birds, taking note of the direction of the wind.

Hunters usually stalk geese after following or spotting a flock during their feeding period, which usually occurs twice daily, once in midmorning and again toward late afternoon. Be prepared to use any available cover to sneak on a flock of geese. Sometimes they will land in a field that is impossible to sneak. Better to find another flock where you are more likely to make a successful stalk.

When geese land in an open field, try team hunting. One hunter hides along an edge of the field, while another approaches from the opposite side. When the birds fly, they may pass over the hiding hunter.

GOOSE DECOY SETS

COMBINATION FIELD. *Place snow goose decoys on the downwind side of the spread. On the upwind side, set your Canada decoys, leaving a large opening. Hide among the snow goose decoys or in a pit blind near the downwind side of the spread and shoot as the geese approach the landing zone from the downwind side.*

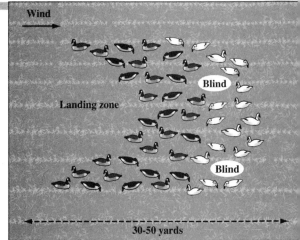

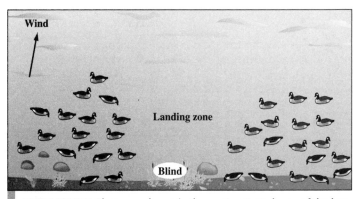

WATER SPREAD. *Place your decoys in the most protected area of the bay, leaving an opening about 15 yards wide for the birds to land in the middle of the spread. The opening should be directly in front of the blind. The outermost decoys should be no more than 35 yards from the blind, giving you a distance guide to approaching geese. Depending on the size of the water you're hunting, you'll need from one to six dozen decoys to hunt geese on the water.*

187

INDEX

Creative Publishing international, Inc. offers a variety of how-to books.
For information write:
Creative Publishing international, Inc.
Subscriber Books
5900 Green Oak Drive
Minnetonka, MN 55343

PHOTO CREDITS

(Note: T=Top, C=Center, B=Bottom, L=Left, R=Right, i=inset)

Charles J. Alsheimer
Bath, NY
© Charles J. Alsheimer: p. 62

Denver Bryan
www.DenverBryan.com
© Denver Bryan: pp. 144, 145

Kathy Butt
Portland, TN
© Kathy Butt: p. 84

Judd Cooney
Pagosa Springs, CO
© Judd Cooney: p. 66

Donald M. Jones
Troy, MT
© Donald M. Jones: pp. 9, 14, 92, 159, 159i

Gary Kramer
Willows, CA
© Gary Kramer: p. 176

Bill Lea
Franklin, NC
© Bill Lea: p. 108-109

Stephen W. Maas
Wyoming, MN
© Stephen W. Maas: pp. 80, 90-91, 97, 100, 172

Bill Marchel
Fort Ripley, MN
© Bill Marchel: pp. 6-7, 146, 151, 168, 177T, 177B, 181T, 184, 185TR, 185BR

Robert McCaw
Moffat, Ontario, Canada
© Robert McCaw: p. 81

Bill McRae
Choteau, MT
© Bill McRae: pp. 10, 33B, 94, 103, 107

Arthur Morris/BIRDS AS ART
Indian Lake Estates, FL
© Arthur Morris: pp. 185BL, 185i

Scott Nielsen
Superior, WI
© Scott Nielsen: pp. 180, 181BL, 181BR

Debi Ottinger
Ridgefield, WA
© Debi Ottinger: cover - B

Bob Robb
Valdez, AK
© Bob Robb: back cover

Ron Spomer
Bloomington, IN
© Ron Spomer: pp. 105, 121, 131, 131i, 142, 143, 185TL

Tom Stack & Associates
Key Largo, FL
© Jeff Foott: p. 114
© Victoria Hurst: cover - TR; pp. 112-113, 119
© Thomas Kitchin: pp. 119i, 127
© John Shaw: p. 137
© Diana L. Stratton: p. 152

Tom Walker
Denali Park, AK
© Tom Walker: p. 122